# DYNAMIC
# YOUTH
# LEADERSHIP

Other titles by Andy Back:

*101 Dynamic Ideas for Your Youth Group*
*Acts of God: The Storyline*
*Dan the Man: The Storyline*

# DYNAMIC
# YOUTH
# LEADERSHIP
## Principles in Practice

# ANDY BACK

**WORD PUBLISHING**

Word (UK) Ltd
Milton Keynes, England
CHRISTIAN MARKETING
Kilsyth, Victoria, Australia
WORD COMMUNICATIONS LTD
Vancouver, B.C., Canada
STRUIK CHRISTIAN BOOKS (PTY) LTD
Maitland, South Africa
ALBY COMMERCIAL ENTERPRISES PTE LTD
Balmoral Road, Singapore
CHRISTIAN MARKETING NEW ZEALAND LTD
Havelock North, New Zealand
JENSCO LTD
Hong Kong
SALVATION BOOK CENTRE
Malaysia

DYNAMIC YOUTH LEADERSHIP

© 1992 Andy Back

Published by Frontier Publishing International in association with
Word Publishing, Milton Keynes, England.

ISBN 0-85009-554-9 (Australia 1-86258-205-X)

Unless otherwise stated, Scripture references are taken from the Holy
Bible, New International Version, copyright © 1973,1978,1984 by
International Bible Society.
Other Scripture references are taken from the New American Standard
Bible (NASB), © the Lockman Foundation, 1960, 1962, 1963, 1968, 1971,
1972, 1973, 1975, 1977.

Reproduced, printed and bound in Great Britain for Word (UK) Ltd. by
Clays Ltd. St Ives plc.

92 93 94 95 / 10 9 8 7 6 5 4 3 2 1

# Acknowledgements

I could not have put pen to paper (or finger to computer keyboard) without the contribution of  past and present members of the team with whom I work at Dunamis. I am particularly grateful to Chris and Debbie Jarvis for their enthusiastic encouragement as I have developed my ministry among teenagers.

To
**Ian Chalmers**
a man whose gentle
and humble teachability
has been a provocation
and encouragement to me.

**Frontier Publishing International** is committed to the production of printed and recorded materials with the view to reaching this generation with the gospel of the kingdom. FPI is part of New Frontiers International, a team ministry led by Terry Virgo, which is involved in planting and equipping churches according to New Testament principles. New Frontiers International is also responsible for a wide range of training programmes and conferences.

# Contents

# Introduction

Your youth group may be small or large; perhaps mostly populated by Christians, or entirely by heathens; with a wide age range, or a strictly defined one. It may meet in a home (even in your own home, if you enjoy living life on the edge) or in a church building, and the group may be difficult to handle, or it may be experiencing revival. Whatever your circumstances, I hope this book will be helpful to you, since I have tried to share my experience in small and large, well-behaved and indisciplined, ungodly and righteous youth groups.

This book does not contain many techniques or formulas, but outlines principles which will apply to groups of any size — although some may need slight adaptation for very small groups. It will help you to become more dynamic as you begin or continue your role in youth leadership.

*Dynamic* is a word which goes some way towards describing the vital characteristics of a youth worker: it has to do with motivation and movement, energy, explosive power and the conserving of energy (the word *dynamo* comes from the same root word — the Greek *dunamis*). I happen to know this because *Dunamis* is the name given to the young teens group at Clarendon Church.

I have worked with Dunamis for several years — four years as a member of the leadership team — and I have picked up many helpful ideas along the way. The guidelines and principles outlined in this volume have all been gathered over years of experience, and sometimes through painful trial and error.

For reasons of clarity and brevity, as well as a genuine desire to be as helpful as possible, I have made some statements which perhaps imply that I took decisions or made pastoral assessments alone. This is certainly not the case; without the team of committed and faithful colleagues with whom I work, my experience would be impoverished. There are a number of real-life situations and examples mentioned in this book, and in order to preserve confidence, I have not used the real names.

My involvement with leading groups of young people began while I was one myself! I was president of my school Christian Union for three years, and went on to work with the Schools Ministry of Agapé for six years. During this time, I worked with teenagers in church youth group settings as well as in evangelistic meetings. Since then, I have rarely been away from youth ministry, and have recently become self-employed in order to have the freedom to exercise my gifting more widely.

Contrary to what you may have been led to believe in the press, this book does not contain any tips about cheap ways to raise South American long-haired oxen. If that's what you'd rather read about, buy *Yak Farming in Bolivia for less than 10 Escudos a Day* by Brian Thug, which, I expect, gives a fuller treatment of the subject.

*Chapter One*

# Calling, Purpose and Vision

This book is designed to equip you for the important work of training young people in their walk with God.

It is about the hard work, and sometimes, the pain of caring for teenagers who may be hurting or confused. It is about communicating God's love for young people. It is about the care we need to take, the joys we can find and the persistence we need to have to minister to these young men and women. They are constantly undergoing change — in their bodies, in their relationships and in their attitudes towards peers, parents, friends and authority.

It is about giving young people a great time, and enjoying yourself thoroughly in the process.

## Calling

It is good to consistently examine the reasons why you are involved in youth work (or the reasons why you want to be). What motivates you? There may be many reasons why you are keen to be involved, but the fundamental reason needs to be that you have been called by God to this work.

Are you excited at the prospect of seeing the young people? Are you glad to see newcomers? Can you remember salient information about individuals? Are you expectant for God to be active in your events, whatever they may be? Can you look back to a time when God specifically quickened these stirrings within you? Or have you always been enthusiastically interested in the lives of young people?

Is there any fruit from your labour? Has anyone become a Christian recently? Have any of the Christians grown as a result of your work? Is their walk with God being strengthened? Do your worship times exalt the name of Jesus? Does the Holy Spirit presence Himself in your teaching? Lack of fruit is, however, often a subjective analysis; so ask others. What do your church leaders and fellow youth workers say about your ministry?

If you know that there are areas where you need to improve, but that generally the answer is 'yes' to many of these pointed questions, then be encouraged. We must take the time and trouble to encourage one another as youth workers, since the enemy will try to attack us all the more if we are bearing fruit. Perhaps it would be helpful for you to talk areas of weakness through with other youth workers or with your church leaders.

The apostle Paul felt he needed to state clearly that God had appointed him to his task, and Jesus Christ, the son of God, was anointed before He undertook His ministry.

> *I thank Christ Jesus our Lord, who has given me strength, that he considered me faithful, appointing me to his service* (1 Tim. 1:12).
>
> *You know what has happened throughout Judea, beginning in Galilee after the baptism that John preached — how God anointed Jesus of Nazareth with the Holy Spirit and power, and how he went around doing good and healing all those who were under the power of the devil, because God was with him* (Acts 10:37,38).

Surely it is unwise of us to expect to be able to serve the Lord without being appointed to the task by God and by our church leaders, or anointed with the Holy Spirit and power to achieve all the good works God has for us to do.

David served his God until the day he died, the Bible says.

> *For when David had served God's purpose in his own generation, he fell asleep; he was buried with his fathers and his body decayed. But the one whom God raised from the dead did not see decay* (Acts 13:36,37).

It is incredible, but true, that the incident with Bathsheba is not even mentioned in the passage in Acts — God promises to forgive us our sins when we repent, and to cast them into the uttermost depths of the ocean and to remember them no more.

So the summary of the man's life could be as sweeping as this: he served the purpose of God in his generation.

I will not content myself with anything less than serving God's purpose in my generation. I am glad to be able to minister to today's young people. But I challenge you to do whatever God has called you to do — to teach, to prophesy, to arrange exciting programmes, to minister in healing, to bring pastoral counsel, to do schools evangelism — or to serve God in another area of church life.

If this demands a change or a radical lifestyle for you to achieve this, then go for it! If God has called you, then consider working part-time, if your financial responsibilities are not too great. Think about giving up every weekend for His service (plan your holidays and rest times well, if you do this). Consider the resources God has made available to you and serve Him with all your might. He is no man's debtor. He is worth everything.

*If anyone serves, he should do it with the strength God provides, so that in all things God may be praised through Jesus Christ. To him be the glory and the power for ever and ever. Amen* (1 Pet. 4:11).

# Purpose

Every time I go to youth group meetings, I try to make sure that my attitude to the young people is positive and helpful, and that we are all expecting things from God. The first priority each time the youth group meets is that God is honoured and that His people give Him room to meet with them.

With any other priorities, we are on shifting sand, and likely to be running a good youth club, at best. I don't have a problem with people running good youth clubs — let's face it, we need to have good youth clubs — but my passion, my calling is to be involved with a youth club which uncompromisingly stands up for the gospel in a way which is relevant, dynamic and palatable for young people.

Getting started, or changing the emphasis your youth group currently has, are tasks which will require enormous effort — and they also need the activity of a gracious, powerful

God. I know from experience that maintaining a youth club which is true to its values is impossible without God's help.

Make a decision that you will set yourself a high goal. Consider the goal Paul set for himself and his fellow-workers.

*We proclaim him, admonishing and teaching everyone with all wisdom, so that we may present everyone perfect in Christ. To this end I labour, struggling with all his energy, which so powerfully works in me* (Col. 1:28,29).

Setting targets such as high numbers, the rapid development of an evangelistic strategy and the purchase of new equipment are all very well, but the main question is this — at the end of the day, what do you want to have achieved? A big crowd? Quality shuttlecocks? Surely the purpose must be to help bring young people into a mature relationship with God, as far as you are able, and with their co-operation.

# Vision

God gives vision to those whom He has chosen to meet a need. This generation needs to see the Christian life lived out; it needs positive role-models; it needs salvation; it needs truth proclaimed and it needs to discover that not all churches are boring, dead places. We have the call of God to bring young people through to maturity in Christ, and thereby we can confront a godless generation with a message of hope. We can be those role-models to the young people in our youth groups, and they can then have a positive influence over their peers. Many will look up to them, and respect them for their Christian stand. And we can give young people a good experience of church life.

I do not want to see young people settle for mere religious form or for ceremony, or for anything less than the real thing. Church life should come complete with New Testament values and activities, teaching the Bible, worshipping the Lord and encouraging spiritual growth and evangelism. My goal is that they never think that it doesn't really matter what sort of church they attend.

Therefore we should aim to have a high level of spiritual activity in our youth group meetings. We are not putting on a scaled-down version of the adult meeting, but a custom-designed mix of worship, teaching, opportunities to exercise spiritual gifts, with prayer, evangelism and a lot of fun. Making the event hilarious or entertaining is not a primary objective; but we do need to be aware of the attention-span of the average teenager. So try to ensure that they are not distracted by more exciting things. After all, it takes a fresh effort of the will every three seconds to concentrate. We need to help our young people to pay full attention to whatever is happening — whether it's a talk, worship, prayer, or simply the rules of a new game or activity.

We must be determined in God to have a high expectation, to plan for numerical growth, to pray for spiritual growth and be confident of our high calling. This may seem rather grand, but the reality is that young lives are changed dramatically when we aim for high standards.

There is great satisfaction in realising that from tentative beginnings, I won Geoff's respect and trust, and was privileged to pray for him to receive the baptism of the Holy Spirit. I have since watched him grow in confidence as now, still only sixteen, he speaks prophetically and powerfully to his peers. I am very glad that Linda trusted me to the extent that she asked me many difficult theological and ethical questions over the four years while she was a Dunamite — giving her confidence as she witnessed to friends at school, and now, at sixth form college. There is a genuine warmth which blesses me when Mike chats to me freely about personal things, since I have worked hard to win the trust of a boy who was once a difficult, riotous young lad.

And few things will beat the delight of praying with young people, and hearing them speak to God with honesty, openness and depth of relationship. If nothing else, I trust that you will catch my excitement for seeing God change young people from death to abundant life, and into extensive ministry and blessing.

## Chapter Two

# Characteristics
# of a Youth Leader

It is vital that we have personal qualities which back up the words we say.

> *Watch your life and doctrine closely. Persevere in them, because if you do, you will save both yourself and your hearers* (1 Tim. 4:16).

Paul exhorts Timothy to be careful about his life, not just his doctrine. If our lives do not match what we say, we not only demonstrate our hypocrisy, but we will lose credibility with those whom we are teaching. We are not going to achieve sinless perfection on this side of glory, but we can be careful to build positive things into our character. This list of fifteen characteristics underlines the importance of sanctification.

## 1. God-fearing

Sometimes it is helpful to take a step back from our desire to serve the Lord and to consider our own relationship with Him. In Isaiah 6, the prophet is suddenly confronted with God in all His glory, and he reacts thus:

> *'Woe to me!' I cried. 'I am ruined! For I am a man of unclean lips ... and my eyes have seen the King, the LORD Almighty'* (Isa. 6:5).

When we understand who God is, we are undone. Our sinfulness cannot stand in the presence of His holiness. Our reaction is to be filled with awe and reverence for this mighty God. This is the amazing truth: God has declared us righteous in Christ (2 Cor. 5:21). He has cleaned our lips, and made us worthy, seeing in us the Lord Jesus in all His purity. We are clothed with righteousness, and we have been declared holy.

The fear of God is something we need to cultivate in our hearts; am I filled with awe in His presence, or have I become too familiar, too free and easy with this mighty God? Of course, we are called into sonship, and we have free access to the throne of God, through the Lord Jesus Christ, with the Spirit interceding; yes, but have we firmly established in our minds the fact that this is the creator God, the Holy One?

Once Isaiah has been undone in God's presence, and confesses his sin, God asks a question:

> *Then I heard the voice of the Lord saying, 'Whom shall I send? And who will go for us?' And I said, 'Here am I. Send me!' He said, 'Go and tell this people ...'* (Isa. 6:8,9).

Isaiah hears the voice of God, and he asks God to send him. Surely this refers to the call of God, to our willingness to do whatever He requires. Isaiah didn't wait to hear what the task might be — in fact, the message is rather bad news — but he was ready to do God's will. And God didn't argue, or make it clear that He'd prefer it if someone more suitable were to go with the message. God saw Isaiah's reverent fear, his confession, and his zeal, and that was sufficient. What does God see when He looks at you? Does He see ambition or casualness? Or does He see in you what He saw in Isaiah?

## 2. Walking consistently with God

If we are people who fear God, and have turned away from our sin, then we must live as people who have turned towards God.

> *... Forgetting what is behind and straining towards what is ahead, I press on towards the goal to win the prize for which God has called me heavenwards in Christ Jesus* (Phil. 3:13,14).

As we put our sinful lives behind us, and leave them there, as it were, forgotten, we give our full attention to the goal. The word translated here *straining* is the same word used to describe a horse, racing at full gallop, his mane and tail flowing, sweat on his flanks, and the rider clinging on for dear life! This is not an image of plodding or gently drifting toward the goal which God has set before us. A good racehorse does not only give his utmost, but he does so throughout the race. It is pointless to put on a sudden burst of effort if you're too far behind to have a hope of catching up the rest of the field! Similarly, there are no prizes for pace-setters who do not stay the course.

Someone once said that the Christian life is more like a marathon than a sprint. Actually, several people have said that, and some of them have said it more than once. But the statement is true.

Why do we press on? To win the prize. Those who walk consistently with God will attain a crown of glory, and will please God. I want to hear God say to me, 'Well done, you good and faithful servant!' I can bring that to pass by letting my life be exposed to the light of God's truth and by giving everything I have for His sake. When my life is tested by fire, I don't want to see wood, hay and stubble going up in smoke, but gold and silver being purified, and precious stones emerging, which will not only please me, but will please God.

How can we walk consistently with the Lord? By spending time with God, reading the Bible, praying, worshipping, and then obeying His Word, putting into practice the lessons learned, and by being filled with the Spirit at all times, listening to Him, and humbly following His way.

*Blessed is the man who does not walk in the counsel of the wicked or stand in the way of sinners or sit in the seat of mockers. But his delight is in the law of the Lord, and on his law he meditates day and night* (Ps. 1:1,2).

We need to be wise about how we spend our time. God's desire is that we give Him our best; reading the Bible, praying, meditating on God's Word ... Too much time spent with unbelievers, and people who are discouraging, cynical or unhelpful can sap our strength and short-circuit our ability to walk consistently with the Lord, as we give in to compromise in our thoughts, or our speech or our activities. But as we give attention to filling our minds with truth and holiness, then the

Spirit of God will affect our attitudes, our words and our behaviour.

## 3. A positive role-model

Jesus points out that we must be willing to set a good example, just as He has done.

> I tell you the truth, no servant is greater than his master, nor is a messenger greater than the one who sent him (John 13:16).

Since Jesus was willing and able to be obedient to God, and to live a life of righteousness and love, we His servants must demonstrate the same willingness to be holy. Young people are looking to Jesus for their example, but they are also following our lead as well. Therefore, we need to have a high standard in order to be setting a good enough example to be worth following. When someone loves God and walks consistently with Him, they will be setting a fine example to the young people. Obviously, outward show alone is ultimately worthless, since teenagers are powerfully gifted with the ability to see through anything which is fake or put on. But be aware that they are watching you and taking a lead from you.

We must recognise that teenagers are especially prone to certain sins, and it is unhelpful for them to see those sins in the lives of their youth leaders. Piling up large debts, gambling, smoking, drinking to excess or the abuse of restricted substances, sexual sin and selfish ambition are all best left behind before a person enters God's service in front of the penetrating gaze of teenagers.

On the positive side, a youth worker should be displaying the fruit of the Spirit, have a healthy prayer-life, maintain control over his or her appearance, habits, language, temper and relationships, and be regularly feeding his or her spirit from the Scripture. The dynamic youth worker is bold in evangelism, exercises the gifts of the Holy Spirit in meetings and elsewhere, and shows appropriate respect towards authority.

Good questions to ask: do you display any of these qualities, to any extent? Are you setting the best example you can, or have your standards slipped a little? Do you allow tiredness to overcome your patience, such that you give in to anger? Are you causing weaker (less mature) brothers and sisters to fall by your freedom to drink or attend discos regularly? Can they handle the pressures found in such activities with the grace and maturity which you have? Do you need to examine the way you interact with the opposite sex?

Be aware that you are being observed: by the young people, who are looking to you for a standard, and for a role-model; and by the Devil, who is prowling around like a roaring lion, looking for someone to devour.

Don't allow carelessness to gain a foothold in your life. Are you giving in to cynicism or unbelief? Have you lost your first love?

## 4. A committed church member

It is important for youth leaders to be setting standards in their attendance of church services and homegroup meetings, as well as in perseverance in attending youth meetings and gatherings of youth workers.

I feel that since we believe that youth work is part of the church, not a bolt-on optional extra, youth workers should be members of the church first, demonstrating a level of commitment to the goals and values of the church and participation in whatever accountability structures may exist (pastoring, discipling, homegroups, local area meetings, or whatever), and then progress to youth work. Since we are desiring to build the church and bring in the kingdom of God, we must be a living part of the church. For some people this will be a natural and assumed part of their lives.

In the church to which I belong, the services are lively, and there is good music, quality time given to worship, opportunities for members to contribute spiritual gifts, and relevant teaching. The homegroup meetings vary in quality, but most are friendly and warm, offering a place for openness and the chance to share God's goodness. The prayer meetings are full as we corporately call on God to pour out His blessing on us as a church, on the town, and to the nations, often all praying out loud simultaneously.

Let's be realistic: I have, in the past, been in church services that were dull, in homegroup events that were intense, and in many prayer meetings that were silent torture. But if the young people in your care are ever to catch the vision of God's plans for His Bride, then they need to see your commitment to being involved with what God is doing in your church.

If your church is really that bad, why have you joined it? I would be loathe to suggest that anyone should leave their church, but, if you cannot really say with integrity that you believe that the church to which you belong is serving the purpose of God in your generation, actively demonstrating the abundance of life of which Jesus spoke, and is making moves towards neither of these tasks, then a move should be on the cards, after loving and honest discussions with those over you in the Lord (homegroup leaders, elders, ministers, etc.).

If, however (as may well be the case), the problem is basically one which has its roots in your preference for youth work in favour of making a contribution to other aspects of church life, then you need to reconsider your motivation. Make an effort to befriend others in the church; it may be that you will get on with people in your homegroup, if you take the trouble to explore any areas of mutual interest.

## 5. A person under authority

There is a whole chapter on the subject of covering and oversight, but the primary question to be faced is: are you willing to submit to spiritual authority?

Jack was a lovable, but slightly difficult young man at the youth group, and, since he was now fourteen, and therefore among the oldest in the group, we thought that one way we could help him to face up to life's realities and responsibilities was to promote him to the role of Junior Leader. This was a dreadful title, but one which set some dozen young people apart from the rest, and gave them various simple duties, such as helping with practical tasks, taking a lead at prayer times and in worship, etc. So Jack was appointed. One club night, he was larking about, and being a nuisance, having to be reprimanded. The next day, at the Junior Leaders' meeting, he asked for the right to punish miscreants. But his problem was that he had first to submit to the authority set over him and be seen to be obedient. He saw the wisdom of this, and his standard of behaviour improved dramatically.

When it comes to youth leaders, we have to submit to those over us in the Lord, and we have to do so willingly, and we have to do so whether they are right or wrong, so long as they are not ungodly. I would even be so bold as to suggest that we should obey decisions when they seem to us to be poor ones. Well, obey them while you see if you can have them changed, by discussing the issues in a polite and helpful manner.

God requires us to resist the temptation to become angry or despondent when we are passed over or not helped as much as we had hoped. We should make our presence felt, especially if there are crying needs which can easily be met by a little time, money or credibility being given to us. But it is really important to demonstrate genuine respect and esteem towards those whom God has appointed.

*Obey your leaders and submit to their authority ... Obey them so that their work will be a joy, not a burden, for that would be of no advantage to you* (Heb. 13:17).

Obey the command of the Lord to obey those authorities. And in time, our respect and esteem may have the effect of changing the hearts of any who have misunderstood or been unhelpful to us and our ministries. My experience (in another church setting) is that church leaders who opposed us were willing to change their opinions when they saw our commitment to what we were doing, the fruit that was coming from it, and that we maintained positive attitudes towards them.

## 6. Filled with the Holy Spirit

I do not have the space here to outline the doctrine of the person and work of the Holy Spirit, so one or two general comments about the baptism or filling of the Holy Spirit will have to suffice.

There are many passages in Acts which show how the

apostles felt about the baptism of the Holy Spirit: they knew it was vital. The work of God in salvation is all that is needed for entry into heaven; but the baptism of the Holy Spirit is needed for holy living and abundant life while still on earth. Jesus was baptised in water, when the Holy Spirit symbolically descended upon Him. He went off to the wilderness and was tempted, and then He returned to Nazareth, and the first words of His teaching ministry (as Luke records it) were: 'The Spirit of the Lord is upon me ...' He was very aware of the ministry and power of the Holy Spirit.

As God restores His church and many find freedom and fullness of life through the baptism of the Holy Spirit, it is important that as youth leaders we are looking to God to empower and anoint us for the work.

The apostle Paul adds this comment:

*Now about spiritual gifts, brothers, I do not want you to be ignorant* (1 Cor. 12:1).

We must not content ourselves with passive observation, or a theoretical awareness of something we dismiss as belonging to a bygone age. I believe that we should be discovering spiritual gifts personally. As youth workers, we should be setting the standard in contributing to the meetings we have with the young people. If their leaders are standing up and speaking out prophetic insights, they will be encouraged to do the same or similar, and there will be an edification of everyone which will obey the Scripture and please the Lord.

There is a whole chapter on the subject of *Charismatic Life* later in the book. Please don't turn to it yet; there's a lot more to read before you get to that, right? Right.

## 7. Willing to work hard

There is little room for the fainthearted in youth work. Someone has to get the table tennis tables out, set up the snooker, provide a football, arrange for the tuck shop, put the hot water on for coffees, run the prayer time, and do all this before the young people arrive. It is discourteous to set up after they have arrived. It is also harder, since they will be in the way, and unable to occupy themselves until things are set up. So do yourself a favour. Anyway, guess who has to do all these tasks, and then put everything away again afterwards? Correct in one.

*We work hard with our own hands ...* (1 Cor. 4:12).

It is a sad fact that teenagers are unable to put sweet wrappers and empty cans in bins, to pick up snooker or ping-pong balls once they have fallen to the floor, to prevent themselves from larking around with toilet paper, or keep quiet in the dark streets outside the building, waiting for lifts home.

Why is it that people with short fuses on their tempers, with offspring who wake at the merest noise, e.g. snowflakes falling gently on moss outside their double-glazed windows, and with completely unreasonable attitudes always rent or buy houses near church buildings? It's one of the little mysteries of the western world.

Please be sympathetic with me; I have been in youth work for a long time, and I do let things get to me now and again.

I know there are some teenagers who use litter bins, clear up after themselves, use washroom facilities only as nature intended, and, when outside, speak in reverent tones, respectful of neighbours. I have met one or two like that, but it's the others who tend to make more impact on the memory, and on the amount of work needed to supervise and maintain a youth group.

It is sheer hard work sometimes to clear up the table tennis tables and waste bins, to hoover the carpet in the tuck shop, and to mop the kitchen floor, especially after a hard night of dealing with disciplinary problems, counselling people with difficulties and leading a meeting. As youth workers, we need to recognise that God is eager to give us patience and strength to do our duties and chores, as well as to help us as we minister.

The hard work is not just physical; there are often situations where I need to work hard in listening to a young person pouring out his heart to me, and in maintaining an unshocked appearance, if necessary.

I do not believe that youth workers should be totally unshockable — the dreadful stories I sometimes hear shock me completely — but I serve the young person well if I do not communicate horror by facial expressions. I often need to talk to other youth workers in order to express my shock or distress at what I have been told.

## 8. Faithful

Youth leaders need to know that the team will arrive in good time, be ready to work hard, be excited about seeing the young people and be expectant for God to move.

One of the keys in our efforts to establish friendships with young people is consistency; therefore faithfulness is an important quality for us to have.

Whatever our talents or abilities, we want to hear the voice of Jesus:

> Well done, good and faithful servant! You have been faithful with a few things; I will put you in charge of many things. Come and share your master's happiness!
> (Matt. 25:23)

I once heard someone say that they were in youth work for the sake of the young people. I agreed to some extent, but the thought occurred to me that I am doing it for Jesus' sake. It is a love-gift to Him that I show up and willingly work as a servant to these young people, that some might be saved, and that some might be brought to maturity in Christ. My motivation keeps me faithful.

As we feed on Christ, allowing His character to abide in us, we will produce good fruit. Faithfulness is part of the fruit of the Spirit (Gal. 5:22) and therefore we can increase our measure of faithfulness by diligently reading the Bible, praying, worshipping and walking closely with God.

As Jesus becomes increasingly important in our lives, His character will be displayed in our lives. That's the amazing promise of God: take hold of it!

> And we, who with unveiled faces all reflect the Lord's glory, are being transformed into his likeness with ever-increasing glory, which comes from the Lord, who is the Spirit (2 Cor. 3:18).

We are being made more like Him as we follow Him. And as we become more like Him, we are being transformed into those who are even more like Him!

## 9. Full of faith

We are not doing youth work for the sake of our health — if we were, we would stop, and do something less stressful, like lion-taming or training to be an air traffic controller. We are youth workers because we have been called to serve the Lord in this field.

One of the key men of the book of Acts, Barnabas, is described thus:

> He was a good man, full of the Holy Spirit and faith, and a great number of people were brought to the Lord (Acts 11:24).

It is interesting that the characteristic of being full of faith is specifically mentioned; presumably he displayed other characteristics and gifting as well, since so many were saved through his ministry. Faith is a gift of the Spirit, which enables us to be sure of what we hope for, and certain of what we do not see (Heb. 11:1).

When we are called by God to do a particular task, we get on with our responsibilities to achieve God's purposes. If God has revealed His will to us, then we must fix our eyes on this and go for it with all our might, not being vaguely laid back and casual.

We must be expectant of the good things God is willing and able to do through us and in the lives of the young people. Since we have been called to this important work, we should be full of faith that God will bring fruitfulness into our ministry.

As with most things, so it is with youth work; there are times when things go well, and times when the going gets tough. We need to exercise faith at all times, but particularly when the work is complicated, unrewarding, going through a season of unfruitfulness or just plain hard graft. The youth worker who is full of faith will not give up, but keep moving steadily towards the goal, seeing the result, not just the obstacles or difficulties.

## 10. A person with a sense of humour

Take this simple test: What do you get if you cross a cow with a hedgehog? A steak with a built-in toothpick.

If you are chuckling away, then you may have a sense of humour, or perhaps you are just a jolly sort of character, or a drooling simpleton. If you are not amused by this joke, please forgive me and try to enjoy life a little more. If you don't understand what all the fuss is about, apply for homegroup leadership instead of youth work.

The important point to all this is that, generally, young people have a very strong sense of humour, and they appreciate a good atmosphere of fun. The ability to be funny and to laugh at their jokes is something which will endear you to them, and them to you, as you interact with and befriend them.

## 11. Adaptable

Since the time of life through which young people are going is a time of change, then the young people may be demanding one week, reluctant to open up another week, and friendly and outgoing another. These are not major character swings, but simply the way life is for these complicated people. We need to be able to allow for this.

Therefore, youth workers need to be able to 'go with the flow' and to be willing to accept the young people where they are. This does not mean compromising on matters of discipline, policy or doctrine, but being aware that puberty, sanctification and becoming mature are all processes, rather than events.

## 12. Forgiving

Mistakes may be made; young people are going through dramatic changes in their whole lives, and therefore they will make mistakes. As youth leaders, we must give them room to make their own mistakes, within reason, because people learn the most from their own experiences, rather than from the things they are told about in unrelated messages.

We have to be able to forgive them, when they let us down, or when they let others down, or when they let themselves down, and when they let the Lord down. Forgiveness is neither easy nor light — it demands that we draw on reserves of grace from God. But true forgiveness leads to life and growth, as the sins are remembered no more, not held against them, or used as ammunition when they next fall.

> *Therefore, I tell you, her many sins have been forgiven — for she loved much. But he who has been forgiven little loves little* (Luke 7:47).

I have been forgiven much. I am aware of God's great mercy shown to me. I am learning how to show great mercy and forgiveness to others.

## 13. Not a figure of fun

Young people are sensitive to those who work with them. The teacher at school who was too old, too unhip, or too strict was quickly singled out and disliked, often mocked behind his back and generally not respected. Come on, admit it, you used to call your least favourite teachers names, didn't you?

True, we were disrespectful to the teachers we did like, too, but it was much healthier than using unkind and disparaging names. I recall a scientist who used hand signals rather too often and was referred to as 'The Thumb'; a modern language teacher who unfortunately had overactive spittle glands who became 'Flobber' Griffiths; and the physics master who grinned as he set fiendish homework was known as 'Smiler' Phillips. Oh, how it all comes flooding back!

But why create difficulties within a youth work team by the kind of people that teenagers fail to respect? I am not referring to minor areas of peculiarity — big noses, hairy warts, baldness — many of us would be disqualified if these were taken into account.

But the unsuitable people in your church who volunteer for almost everything in sight, hoping to find a team where they will be accepted, should be gently turned away from youth work, since the teenagers can be merciless in their teasing, and it is good to avoid giving them a butt for their jokes. No one is served by this sort of situation.

## 14. Appreciative of youth culture

It is vital to be aware of what young people like, even if it is not to your particular taste. When you sit through a whole episode of the trendiest soap opera, or a programme of pop videos, you certainly should find it worrying that young people are exposed to sexually-oriented lyrics and images, and scenes of domestic violence or bad language or whatever. But you should not be surprised.

It is unusual for someone to be a good youth leader and yet strongly dislike all pop music, all modern cinema, all soap operas and all youth fashions. I would guess it was possible, but some of the barriers might be difficult to overcome. The young people will quickly be warned off asking your opinion, if the only answer they ever get is a negative one.

The barriers unwittingly built by a youth worker who has no appreciation of youth culture may be insurmountable. Please be aware that I am using the word *appreciate* because there are things about youth culture we ought not to like or enjoy; but it is important to react positively whenever we can do so without compromising the truth.

## 15. A friend

I am talking here about fellowship between Christians, and genuine friendship between youth workers and young people.

*Now that you have purified yourselves by obeying the truth so that you have sincere love for your brothers, love one another deeply, from the heart* (1 Pet. 1:22).

Youth work is not, as we have seen, just about filling young heads with knowledge about Jesus. It is an adventure in living, a journey together through the things God is revealing. Of course, it is vital that as leaders we take the lead, but there should always be an 'older brother' or 'older sister' part to our relationship with the youngsters.

I feel there is little need for us to 'come down to their level', since often it is more a matter of moving up to their level of freshness and reality in their walk with God, which is expressed in less complicated terms.

I consider many youngsters my friends; and they are obviously comfortable with me, since we may from time to time go out as a crowd and do something fun together. Larry is keen for me to listen to his latest CDs, and to attempt to educate me musically. Paul keeps me up-to-date with the latest jokes. I am genuinely interested in what is happening for Sarah and Tim as they progress through the sixth form. These are young people who have grown beyond the age range of the youth group; our friendships transcend the boundaries of 'youth work' and overflow into normal everyday life. I don't have to pretend to be pleased to see them; our relationship is real.

# Conclusion

To find people who perfectly fulfil all fifteen characteristics may take beyond forever. But it is better to aim high, and recognise that some areas of weakness in you and your team may be overcome by disciplined effort. Setting a high standard seems a better starting point than having a too-low standard and regretting it.

When young people spend regular time with adults who are fun, friendly, Godly, consistent, full of the Holy Spirit, hard-working, faithful, expectant, flexible and the sort of person they want to respect, and even emulate, then they have a good chance of growing up into people with similar characteristics. There is much more likelihood of young people walking with God and becoming strong in their faith if they are nurtured and befriended by someone who has taken the time and trouble to ensure that they are displaying these characteristics.

Determine before God that you will face this challenge and have an influence of excellence over a generation! Where there are areas of weakness, ask someone you respect in the Lord to help you, disciple you, and give you accountability, so that you can be the very best for God's sake.

## Chapter Three
# Strong Team and Dynamic Leadership

Whatever the size of your youth group, I feel it is unwise to have just one person solely responsible for all the ideas, teaching, co-ordination with church leaders, discipline, counselling, practical administration, parent liaison, running the meeting and clearing up afterwards.

This is too much for one person to handle. And it is vital that the males in your youth group have male leaders with whom they can relate, and that the females have female leaders.

No one person can fulfil this criteria. Besides, if you are the only person 'on duty' every time the group meets, you will rapidly run out of vision, encouragement and enthusiasm. It takes two, at least! Equally, it is unhelpful to give all the leadership responsibilities to one person. One of the distinctive features of the charismatic movement has been the return to leadership teams, avoiding the danger of placing all the burden on one pair of shoulders.

> ... Jesus went out to a mountainside to pray, and spent the night praying to God. When morning came, he called his disciples to him and chose twelve of them, whom he also designated apostles (Luke 6:12,13).

The Lord did not have any problem about being exclusive; He knew the people who were suitable for the tasks He had for them and He built His team accordingly.

Some people were left out of the twelve, deemed unsuitable by Jesus, who nevertheless included the thief, liar and betrayer Judas in His selection. Team selection is about picking the best, most suitable and God-appointed characters for the team.

# Leadership team

A ratio of one team member to ten young people is probably very workable, although resources can be stretched when it comes to counselling, personal interaction and other areas of ministry. It is not always possible, I realise, but it is certainly better to have a large team, so that when team members take a week off, or are sick, the gap can be filled relatively easily.

But with a large-ish team, the need for good leadership is more acutely felt. The Bible does not endorse the concept of democracy, or of decisions by committee, and yet it teaches that leadership should be plural, not just one leader making all the decisions. Therefore, a small leadership team is appropriate, designed to prevent imbalance or preference, and which can more easily manage the complexities of running a large youth group.

Work hard to create a structure which will work whether 5, 50 or 250 youngsters turn up, with activities and ministry responsibilities divided among the leadership team.

I am firmly convinced that leaders of youth groups should, wherever possible, be married. I realise that there are relatively few instances where both husband and wife are gifted and called, and where family commitments allow regular involvement. Nevertheless, there is an implied protection for young teens in the married status of the leader. Parents can be suspicious of youth leaders (and in today's social climate, I can see their point of view), and single leaders are more vulnerable to accusation.

In Dunamis, the leader, along with his wife, has oversight of the work. The responsibility to the church leaders and before God rests with him, and therefore, his is the final decision. However, as a leadership team, we have collective responsibility for any decision. So if it's good, we all take the credit, and if it's duff, we can blame him(!)

The leadership team is corporately responsible for: practical tasks, such as the purchase, repair and storage of equipment; assigning team members to their tasks each week; overseeing the teaching programme; team training; ensuring the proper development of worship; counselling and the pastoral covering of young people; talking with candidates for baptism; giving help and guidance to other team members as they develop their abilities to teach, run small groups and lead worship; being the authority figures when disciplinary issues are raised.

# Weekly bulletin

Everything will fall to the ground if there is no effective means of communication between the leaders and the rest of the team. The Team Bulletin, a weekly round-up of admin, news and prayer topics serves the purpose.

This sounds amazingly over the top, but when we have tried to do without this, the second law of thermodynamics goes into operation. Things tend to become chaotic, even though they may have started in very good order. My desk is a prime example of this natural law; if I do not impose order on it at least once a week, things get lost or forgotten. Similarly, even though your youth group may be well-organised, the fact is that havoc will reign very soon if communication and organisation are not adequately maintained.

It takes a long time to prepare the bulletin, and it is expensive to distribute, but when you have a large team, it is vital that every member of the team knows what went on last week, and the plans for next week.

For example, a team bulletin may contain the following information: a report on last weekend's meetings; news of any individual who received salvation, baptism in the Holy Spirit, counsel, healing prayer or a disciplinary ban; pastoral information about young people in our care; team news; details of the plan for next Saturday and Sunday; jokes, puzzles, quotes of the week and other nonsense; and the famed Responsibilities Sheet.

This contains full details of which team member is responsible for which activity or task. Having a large youth group means that a lot of options are provided for the young people, and that generates a lot of jobs: opening the doors; keeping the register and circulating the guest book; supervision; overseeing the tuckshop; floating (moving around the building, discouraging hooliganism and loitering in the corridors and toilets); giving out any leaflets at departure times; clearing up;

and disposing of the eighteen tons of litter.

Without this sheet, as they say, 'Everyone leaves it to Someone, or even Anyone, and eventually No one does it!' Knowing that all the angles are covered, the team have the freedom to concentrate on what they are supposed to be doing.

The bulletin also contains details of the up-front activities each week. The leaders decide who will be leading worship and teaching, and then provide guidelines for the teaching programme. Another team member organises the musicians, and often arranges for people to come in to the meeting to play for our worship time.

Of course, the whole point of this is organisation and communication. You may not need to go to these lengths if you have a small team of youth workers, but the principles here are of paramount importance.

# Team recruitment

The general tendency within Christian work is that there are always more jobs available than those willing or able to fill them. Unemployment is rare; overwork is almost seen as necessary to your salvation. There have been many schemes designed to recruit members of the church to the team of youth workers, and only some of them have borne any fruit. General appeals to the church lack the precise targeting required — well-meaning unsuitables appear in droves, while those whom God is calling don't pay attention during the notices. This is a generalisation, I agree.

So, it often boils down to a two-pronged attack. One of the leaders may attend the church membership course, and appeal to any who have served in youth work before, or who feel this is the direction in which they feel God is leading them, so that they have the opportunity to make themselves known and open the discussion.

Alternatively, specific church members may be invited to consider joining the team.

This invitation is usually based on observation of them in other settings, and can be something of a wild guess, in some cases. Therefore there needs to be a quality control system built in to help us recognise those whom God is calling to be involved in youth work.

# The month of trial

Suppose a young man by the name of Harry has expressed interest in becoming a youth worker. It would be great if someone fully displayed all the characteristics listed in chapter two, but most of the people like that get snapped up for eldership pretty quickly! So we follow this routine. There are a number of basic ground rules:

- Team members must be church members.
- They must be actively involved in the life of the church, i.e. regularly attending Sunday meetings and midweek homegroups, etc.
- The people in immediate pastoral oversight of them must broadly agree with the idea of them serving the church in this way.
- They must be able to serve consistently for a given period of time — I suggest six months is the minimum commitment, since they may take some time to get to know young people and win their confidence.

The rules would disbar Harry if he was not a member of the church, or if he was about to change jobs and move to Blackburn. What the Moses are you applying for, you hooligan? Also, they make sure that the team does not consist of those who may prove to be poor role-models for the young people. Personally, I would prefer to be sure that Harry has been baptised in the Holy Spirit, as well. If he is going to be asked to minister to the young people, he ought to be gifted for the task. However, I am sure that there have been many who would not claim to have been baptised in the Holy Spirit, but who have been greatly used by God to serve young people.

Checking these things out with church leaders can take a week or so, and this stage has been invaluable in weeding out unsuitable people, or those more suited to another area of service in the church. It's unlikely, but perhaps Harry is about to be called by the church leaders to go to Bootle to plant a church or something!

Following the check-out, if Harry is thought suitable, he is informed about the Month of Trial. This sounds worse than it really is! Referred to as the MoT for reasons of convenience and jolly humour, it is a trial period for Harry to get to know some of the young people and to discover what the youth group is all about — what happens, how things are done — and it is an opportunity for the young people to see Harry and to get to know him.

We make it clear what is expected of Harry — he should arrive early and leave late; spend time getting to know a few of the young men; join in with practical and spiritual tasks; realise that the time for chatting to team members is after the young people have gone, not during the evening; and so on. It sounds a bit rigid, but new team members must learn quickly that the youth group is run for the good of the young people, not for the pleasure of the team!

On the first of the four Saturday evenings Harry attends, a youth worker shows him around, and introduces him to some of the young people. The leadership team makes a special point of observing how well he fits in.

Does he make friends easily with some of the lads? Is he overfamiliar with the girls? Does he relate to a broad range of young people or just to the younger ones or the intelligent ones? Does he make an effort to set things up and to clear away afterwards? Does he get stuck in with practical tasks? Is he active when there is a need for team members to intervene spiritually, in praying or ministering to young people? Is he more interested in the young people or in team members?

Harry can make his mind up, too. The MoT may confirm his calling and desire to work with young teens. He may feel more drawn towards another age group, or he may discover that, actually, he would prefer to watch Jeremy Beadle.

The MoT gives him a chance to see for himself, and to make an informed decision about joining the team before he commits himself. Following prayer and discussions among the leadership team, the decision is made, and Harry may receive one of four letters.

- He may be invited to join the team, and be reminded to be alert to any areas of deficiency which have been observed. This may be such things as punctuality, chatting to team members, befriending young people, or whatever.
- He may be advised to seek to serve God in another area of church life. For some, this will be with a different age group, while for others, an area of service outside the children and youth department.
- He may be asked to delay his involvement in this area of service for some reason, e.g. until some pastoral matter relating to his ability to be a positive role-model is resolved, or until he is able to change his shifts to allow him to be regular in attendance.
- He may be told to go and stick his head in a bucket of rancid peanut butter. We have never yet issued such a letter, because we are lovely people, but there's always a first time.

## What being a team member involves

When Harry joins the team, he will be required to attend the monthly team meeting, where news and prayer topics are shared, and where training takes place or reminders about various aspects of youth work are shared. For example, discipline, ministering the baptism of the Holy Spirit, an overview on how to deal with victims of abuse, pastoral care, sexuality, etc. Team members are given the opportunity to ask questions about recent or forthcoming events, and to spend time in prayer together for the young people, for ourselves and for revival to fall on schools in the area.

He is expected to be present whenever youth events happen. This means every Saturday evening, two out of every four Sunday mornings (he can attend the evening service on the Sundays he is on duty), plus holidays, special events and Bible Weeks. Obviously, this is not mandatory; there is sufficient flexibility to allow team members to give notice of any dates when they will be absent, for holidays, or suchlike. The reason for such a high level of commitment is because, to restate a foundational principle, young people need consistency. If team members are establishing relationships with youngsters, then they need to be around. If the teens are less than regular in their attendance, then it could happen that a team member will see them very infrequently, if their absences coincide with the teens' attendances, and vice versa.

When it comes to the general management of team members, then encouragement is the key, alongside motivation by grace. Cracking the whip is not possible with volunteers; and it is less than effective in Christian ministry. But when there is the need to strongly counter any inappropriate behaviour or style of approach to responsibilities, then we must do so for the sake of the kingdom of God. We do not have the right to be rude, but the needs of the furtherance of the kingdom of God must take priority over being nice to someone and refraining from mentioning wrong actions, poor attitudes or bad decisions. If, as youth leaders, we do not speak to the team member in this way, we are failing in our duty of care towards the young people in our group, failing to uphold the good name of the church, and failing to act responsibly as God's chosen stewards of this ministry.

Having a strong team and effective leadership means that the youth group has room to grow, and will keep the leaders from overwork. When there are more people available to do the practical tasks, everyone has more time for the spiritual activities — prayer, study, maintaining your walk with God, more prayer and counselling.

## Chapter Four
# Covering and Back-Up

I have already discussed at some length the role of church leaders in youth work. They need to know what your youth group plans and activities are all about, so that they can provide constant encouragement and wise oversight. In some churches, the policy and direction of the youth work will be adequately mapped out by the leadership; in others, the youth leaders will have to communicate the vision to the church leaders.

Not only is it vital that youth leaders and workers are called, but it is also necessary to know that we are valued by church leaders.

It is equally important that youth leaders and their workers respect the leaders of the church.

*The elders who direct the affairs of the church well are worthy of double honour ...* (1 Tim. 5:17).

Since Paul says that we should be twice as respectful to elders who serve with excellence ('didn't he do well?'), then it follows that we should still give honour to elders who perform less well then we had hoped, or if they have failings, preferences or weaknesses.

Moaning and complaining is destructive — it is far better to pray. We should be working together with the leaders of the church, because we all have the same goal.

Let's not forget that if a young man becomes a Christian, then he is welcomed into the body of Christ, his name is written in the Lamb's Book of Life, Jesus prepares him a place in His Father's mansion, but the local church may effectively bar him from any form of active membership until he is eighteen. So the youth leader is often the main point of contact between the youthful Christian and the church. Let's be good ambassadors!

# Maturity and authority

When a church leader gets thoroughly involved in youth work, and takes an oversight role seriously, his presence imparts a wide range of benefits to the youth group, even if the young people never lay eyes on him. Quality oversight gives stability to a youth group's leaders. Knowing that there is someone on whom you can depend, when all around you is changing, is one of most important aspects of fighting the spiritual battle. Obviously, the Lord is unchanging, but it is great to be able to call for help from a wise overseer. Due to the nature of youth work, sometimes there can be a lack of age and experience in a youth work team — a pastor can redress the balance and bring a level of maturity.

Overseers add the weight of authority to youth leaders, especially when there are unpopular tasks to be carried out by the team. They are available for counsel, control, and they provide safeguards. Youth leaders can sometimes get a bee in their bonnets about certain aspects of the work, and it is helpful to have someone who will exert a steadying influence and bring correction.

Having someone in a church leadership position overseeing the work can also more readily release finance to the group. Budgets and cashflow analyses are not my strong point, but there are definite benefits to having plenty of money to splash around, especially when you want to take the group on a coach to Alton Towers, or to a Bible Week, or on an evangelistic venture. Money also pays for such things as prizes, refreshments on Family Evenings, new equipment, repairs to broken equipment (all snooker tables in every youth group throughout the known world are constantly in need of repair), replacement badminton rackets, video rental, stocking the tuck shop, etc.

There may be times when the youth leader cannot adequately handle difficult pastoral situations alone, due to the scale of the problem, a lack of responsiveness in the individuals concerned, or something outside of the youth leader's experience. For example, God revealed, through a word of knowledge at a youth group meeting, that a teenage girl was depressed due to the constant rows of her parents. When the girl identified herself, she proved to be the daughter of church members. This seemed to be an insurmountable problem, since it is not appropriate for youth leaders to confront parents over an issue like this. So the details were passed on to the elder who was overseeing the youth work at the time, and he followed it through with the parents, which took the pressure off the teenagers.

Similarly, there was an ongoing discipline difficulty from a teenage girl who had been adopted into a fine Christian family. She was adopted as a baby, but she was proving to be troublesome as a teenager, hurting her adoptive parents with claims that she wanted to see her real mother, that she felt unloved, that she didn't belong and that she was a second-class member of the family, compared with her brothers. This was an effective cry for help and attention, but she failed, initially, to respond positively to the counsel and advice which were given. So the elder was asked to get involved, and he took the situation on, set up suitable, trained counselling for the teenage girl, gave encouragement to the parents, and ministered reconciliation within the family.

I suppose that the kind of issues which arise where overseers may be called in are: addictions to drugs, alcohol or glue; sexual immorality — especially where there may be pregnancy or the threat of it, or of sexually transmitted diseases; serious crime; encounters with the demonic; or runaways.

The saddest young people run away from home; either things have become too 'heavy' for them to handle (pressure from rows, overbearing fathers, addictions, violence in the home, etc.), or they have done something so terrible that they cannot face their parents (become pregnant, had an abortion, contracted HIV+, become addicted to something, stolen or simply fallen away from faith). Parents ought never to become unapproachable, but in some situations they do, perhaps through failing to allow their offspring to grow up, find their feet and spread their wings.

The elder's ability to communicate with young people is vital in these situations; a reproachful style is very unhelpful; and so is siding with the runaway. It is more than I could manage to handle, but God is generous and anoints some for these kinds of tasks.

In summary, church leaders, called to the work of

shepherding the flock of God can bring encouragement, wise oversight, stability, maturity, authority, and can also release finances into youth work, as well as be a resource for pastoral problem-solving. Vital, indeed!

However, there may be some youth workers who are faced with difficult or unhelpful church leaders, who have little understanding of young people, and less time for them. I sympathise with you, although perhaps you need to look carefully at the life-expectancy of the youth group if there is no support from the church leaders.

God is all-powerful, and He is also all-knowing, and will vindicate prayerful and careful attempts to serve the young people. God is neither surprised nor thwarted by the situation in which you find yourself. Circumstances can be changed by His mighty power in the twinkling of an eye.

# Chapter Five
# Living in the Promise

Doubtless these comments will upset some people, but it seems to me that God designed the human being to grow up.

We spend a number of years as a child, learning things like walking, co-ordination, focusing our eyes, speaking, playing, running, jumping, and being childish in our irresponsibility, ways of thinking and submission to our parents. Later on, we are adult, with responsibilities, maturity, independence, the ability to make decisions for ourselves, counting the cost and anticipating many of the consequences, etc.

But in between, there is a strange and dangerous place beset with pitfalls, dangers and snares, as if life were out to trip us up, make fools of us and belittle us at the time when we most need to be valued, built-up, esteemed, recognised and loved. This is often called adolescence. It's a very disconcerting place to inhabit.

Everything within you screams for freedom and independence, yet those in authority over you seem to be increasingly unreasonable and restrictive. You want to love them as you always have, but they seem to be down on you all the time. School's the same, with foolish rules and even more foolish teachers, trying to teach you things you learned years ago, and then rushing on, leaving you behind. Having to wear a uniform isn't fair, since other schools are more liberal.

It seems that everyone you respect hates everything you like — your taste in clothes, music, friends and places to meet. So your respect for them begins to be eroded.

Your body explodes in all directions, with strange hormones rushing around, wondering when (if ever) they will get the chance to 'do their thing'. You have suddenly noticed the opposite sex! Girls realise that boys are not just daft, childish oiks who ride bikes and play football all the time, but that they are nicely shaped and can be fun to be around. The boys are noticing that those annoying girls with their squeaky voices and preference for giggling and skipping are becoming very nicely shaped and fun to be with, even though it's somehow nerve-racking, too.

And then it happens. Acne! Just when you realise you need to be attractive to the opposite sex, you burst out in hideous eruptions — scabs and blotches everywhere, but, worst of all, over at least 80 per cent of the surface area of your face.

Schools call it childhood. So do bus companies, swimming pools and many churches. But childhood it ain't. If childhood were like this, none of us would live beyond the age of five without going stark staring bonkers. No one needs more careful, gentle, understanding treatment than a teenager, an adolescent, a nearly-adult, a dweller in this lonely and insecure place, living in the promise of adulthood.

## Treat young people as nearly-adults

If you have a mental picture of something, that's how you will treat it. I know my car, and I know where the clutch 'bites' and the strength of the brakes. But since driving is a skill learned through experience until it becomes almost second nature, when I drive another car, I may stall or brake too fiercely before I become accustomed to that different vehicle.

It is the same with young people. One fifteen-year-old may be childish, while an eleven-year-old may behave in a much more mature way. And individuals can change dramatically from week to week. Some may even change their approach during the course of the club meeting!

It saddens me to hear schoolteachers referring to eleven-year-olds as children. If you treat them as children, they will behave like children. If you treat them as nearly-adults, they may sometimes still behave like children, but at other times, they will surprise you with their maturity, sense of adventure and adaptability.

Take twelve-year-old Kevin, for instance. Kevin's family background is such that he has to fight for survival, let alone attention. Yet when Gary, another twelve-year-old lad came to the club for the first time, Kevin latched onto him, showed him around the facilities, looked after him — even sat next to him in the meeting. Amazing enough — but Gary has a disability which means he walks with two sticks. It was touching to see the two chaps playing table-tennis, and to watch Kevin running to fetch the ping-pong ball. Gary's lack of co-ordination meant the game was a very one-sided event, but Kevin didn't seem to mind. My expectation had been that Kevin would be among a crowd who would jeer and mock Gary's ungainly progress across the hall. Perhaps having the chance to be a somebody for a while meant a lot to Kevin.

This perhaps goes some way towards explaining why I take care to refer to young people as young people, because I do not believe that they are children. They are capable of a lot more than children, though they sometimes (often!) do not choose to exercise their maturity.

The key factor, it seems to me, in the misunderstandings between young teens and their parents is a lack of recognition of this not-quite-but-a-jolly-sight-nearlier-than-you-think middle ground. Many teenagers are insecure and have low self-esteem. They agree with the teachers and parents who constantly get on their backs. They really think they are lazy or good for nothing. They know they 'could try harder', but why bother when there is little reward? They want to be free, but they are required to obey what seem like petty rules and regulations.

Good questions, such as 'Why?' are met with weak answers, such as 'Because I'm your father, and while you're living in my house, you'll do as I say.' This seems to me to be a true statement of reality, and an assertion of appropriate authority, but a comment guaranteed to build barriers, designed to emphasise the difference between adult and offspring, between master and minion. I humbly offer my opinion that a reasoned, friendly approach, full of grace and esteem, would be more effective in the long term.

There are dangers with treating young people as nearly-adults. Some will take advantage of this and push their luck as far as it will go, until your patience runs out. When it does, it tends to snap, rather than just unravel, and then there can be anger and regrettable incidents. Other young people do not behave like adults at all, and are simply childish and immature in their approach. But these exceptions should not mean that we shirk our responsibility to help these youngsters to take hold of adulthood, with all its pressures and pleasures. As we see these children becoming adults, we can forget that there is still a long way to go before we can treat them as peers. Some young people do not have the maturity to maintain confidences, for example.

We must be careful, I feel, to avoid too much physical contact with young people. They are becoming sexually aware and they are extremely alert to signals, whether they are intentional or not. Let us take care not to cause confusion or pressure. Some youngsters are so bewildered about their sexuality that they can believe they are in love with youth leaders — it's not only teachers who can be the subjects of crushes.

Teenage years are years full of insecurity, because it seems that everything is in flux and unreliable. Along with physical, psychological, social and perhaps spiritual change as they mature in their walk with the Lord and give up some sins, there is also a major change in the way others treat them or look on them. Some view teenagers with suspicion (fear of the unknown?) and others continue to treat them as children (crime of crimes, as I've already pointed out).

## Building it into the programme

We can set about the task of running a youth group, and treating the participants as nearly-adults, by incorporating elements into the programme which meet the needs and emphasise the particular strengths of the age group — a pop quiz, or a highly competitive game; perhaps the chance to design your own pizza or discuss a moral issue such as homelessness; a lively time of worship or a talk on being a good witness at school. While they will enjoy the youthful aspects of the activity, they will be learning about relating to one another or to God as adults.

A programme of team-games and eating jelly is too childish for most teenagers unless you have a competition to see which team can construct the most original-looking jelly trifle using the cream that squirts out of the can, cherries, hundreds and thousands, chocolate vermicelli, etc. Equally, an evening set aside for an extended study of a chapter of Leviticus, which may excite some adults, will not appeal very strongly (or be of much help) to a group of teenagers. A short talk about God's desire for us to be holy and set apart from the world (surely one of the applications from the book of Leviticus), followed by prayer in small groups for each other may be of more value.

As in all aspects of Christian work, the key is encouragement. Too much correction or focusing on weaknesses can bring defeat into our lives, while esteem-building comments and public acknowledgement of good characteristics does everyone the power of good.

One of the best systems of training is

- Show them what to do.
- Get them to do it, while you supervise, until they get it right.
- Let them do it unaided.

This system is certainly appropriate for the training of young adults, since we are in the process of helping them become adults.

*Train a child in the way he should go, and when he is old he will not turn from it* (Prov. 22:6).

Surely, the way to train the 'children' in our care is to demonstrate to them how to behave as adults, and then to encourage them to behave that way themselves. This may mean taking a risk or two as you give away responsibility. By the way, to give responsibility without providing accountability is a recipe for disaster, so be careful to supervise with wisdom and willingness to step in when it is needed.

Recently, this was put to the test as I set up a series of *Young People's Seminars*, where three of the more mature teenagers were each asked to prepare a ten-minute seminar on certain subjects. They were coached a little, and encouraged as their preparation went along, and then, one evening, the young people were divided into three groups, and each small group attended each of the three seminars. The speakers had three opportunities to speak, thus polishing their style, getting over nerves and beginning to enjoy themselves; the young people had the pleasure of listening to their peers speaking; and the youth workers had a chance to relax, while others did the teaching.

It was a great success, and all were encouraged, and the quality of the seminars was surprisingly high, with plenty of Bible verses and very little unsupported opinion. But the real benefit came through acknowledging that these particular young people were capable of having a go at what had, up until then, been tasks allocated to adults. Their maturity was respected, and they held their heads high among their peers and the team.

Okay, so none of them turned out to be amazingly gifted as speakers; but they were a lot better than I thought they might be. They were given a chance to show that they were able to do the job, and others asked if they could be given a chance, too.

## Chapter Six
# Meeting their Needs

We all have deep needs. We all need to feel secure. It is vital to know that the rug will not be pulled out from under you and that no one will move the goalposts — whatever metaphor you choose, we need to be secure.

> *Do not let your hearts be troubled. Trust in God; trust also in me* (John 14:1).

Jesus was surely building assurance into the disciples as He spoke of the certain house that the Father has prepared for us. This gives us the freedom to express ourselves and to be relaxed.

We all need to know that we are significant. If I don't really count, then I become despondent, and I will be half-hearted. On the other hand, when I know I am loved, accepted and respected, then I will do my utmost and make every effort to be an achiever and a winner.

> *Therefore, among God's churches we boast about your perseverance and faith in all the persecutions and trials you are enduring* (2 Thess. 1:4).

Paul's words must have raised any drooping heads among the Thessalonians, and encouraged them to consider how important they were, simply by their faith and endurance!

We all need to have self-worth. It is vital that we understand our place in Christ, and have a right appraisal of ourselves.

> *. . . Do not think of yourself more highly than you ought, but rather think of yourself with sober judgement, in accordance with the measure of faith God has given you* (Rom. 12:3).

'Sober judgement' means that we should avoid both pride and self-debasement. It is inappropriate for us to be taken up with ourselves (either positively or negatively). We should fix our eyes on Jesus, and live in accordance with His appraisal of us — we are beloved, clothed with righteousness, ones to whom mercy has been shown, part of His body, and those who have been redeemed from judgement and hell. Another aspect of self-worth is having respect for ourselves, so that we are not always putting ourselves down, volunteering for the grotty jobs, or expecting to be passed over.

So we all have these three basic needs: to be secure, to have significance, and to have self-worth. Having thought about this, I conclude that we all have four needs — we need to eat chocolate, too.

But it is important that we know the specific needs of the young people for whom we care, so that we can bring good counsel, and avoid adding to their hurts and difficulties. It is also vital to let the young people know that when it seems we are being harsh or unaware of their preferences or choices, we have their best interests at heart.

## Salvation

Until we are thoroughly convinced of our need of Christ, we shall never see how important it is for people to be saved.

*You see, at just the right time, when we were still powerless, Christ died for the ungodly* (Rom. 5:6).

The state of the unregenerate person is powerlessness. They are dead in their sins, and perishing as they head towards a Godless eternity. Without a message of hope and light, we are simply helping young people to have a slightly less hideous time while they are alive. Ping-pong alone isn't going to do them much good.

Explaining the good news to a young person is a delicate task, but one which we must undertake with passion and boldness. I think it is vital to explain the gospel to non-Christian young people who come to the youth group, and to give them an opportunity to respond. But this would be rather pressured and predictable if it happened very week. Once a month is sufficient, since any young person who comes to the club meeting will hear something of the good news every week, but if they come for four weeks, they will be challenged to respond at some time during that period. Those who are seriously seeking God will attend the club night, and will ask questions, and many of these will become Christians as they understand the gospel and as the Spirit draws them.

Those who are not really interested either drift away after one or two visits, or they will have to resist the offer of new life on a regular basis. After six months, if it is clear that they are not 'ripe fruit', invite them to go to another youth group until such time as they want to investigate God and His claims on their lives again.

Leading a young person to salvation is an exciting process, beset with pitfalls if we are too eager or careless, but sparkling with delights as God lovingly draws sinners to repentance.

An evangelistic message can certainly be followed by a call to respond, and an invitation to stand or come forward, depending on the size of the meeting. But thereafter, it is best to give each young person individual attention, to answer any questions, and to clarify anything which may have been misunderstood. We should get away from the hubbub, not necessarily in a back room, but at least away from the gaze of others. Speak to those who want to become Christians one at a time; if others have to wait, let them wait — give each one your undivided attention. If they wish, allow a saved friend of theirs to sit with you, but don't attempt to lead two or three to salvation at once, because each one has specific needs. But I strongly suggest that same-sex counselling is a good practice — this avoids some of the many potential difficulties, and is more appropriate if any specific sins are being confessed.

My belief is that a non-Christian needs to recognise the seriousness of sin before forgiveness will make much sense; therefore be clear about what sin is, that being sorry may not be enough (we have to repent), and that God's love cost Jesus everything.

I can happily recommend some materials which help in sharing the good news: for younger people, the *Father God I Wonder* booklets, produced by the Glorie Company, are clear and simple; while older teenagers can be helped by either

*Knowing God Personally*, produced by Agapé, or *Bridge to Life*, produced by the Navigators. Since 'one in the eye is worth four in the ear' (20 per cent of information is received by hearing, while 80 per cent is received by sight), it is very worthwhile to have a pictorial or visual resource to help keep attention, and to clarify the message.

There is an important distinction between understanding and revelation. I do not suppose that every sinner fully understands all the glorious truth of the new birth, but I expect that he will have some measure of revelation about his own state of sinfulness, his need of salvation, and some gratitude for the forgiveness Christ offers. It may help you to be sure about a person's readiness to pray if you ask them what sort of things they want to say to Jesus; if they forget about confessing their sins, or about asking Him for forgiveness, then this may be a pointer to suggest that they have not grasped the essential truths.

By the way, it seems to me to be inadequate to ask Jesus for forgiveness of sins; He is more concerned about the sinful nature of the heart, not just the symptoms of the disease. He wants to deal with sin, not just sins. Therefore, we need to teach young people about becoming a new creation, as well as about the forgiveness of sins.

It is only fair to let a young person know beforehand what the prayer for salvation will contain, so they can decide whether they are ready to pray it or not. This is why it is very helpful to have a printed version of the prayer in front of both of you. Remember, it is not the prayer that saves them, but God, when He sees true repentance in their heart. Ask them to repeat aloud each phrase as you say it, and then rejoice with them in their salvation. This is a suggested prayer:

*Lord Jesus, I realise that I am a sinner, and that I have been running my own life. I am sorry for the wrong things I have done, and I ask you now to forgive me. Thank you for dying on the cross in my place. I now turn away from my sinful life. Please help me to live for you. Amen.*

Follow through effectively — it is not too much to drop the young person a letter during the week, encouraging them to pray and read the Bible — and certainly speak to them at length the next time you see them, answering questions or clarifying points.

A final word of caution: don't be too quick to publicly acknowledge conversion. I have known one or two who 'became Christians' — in reality all they did was pray a prayer and then forget about it.

## Assurance

We have all met people who perform the religious rigmarole, go through ceremonies, and live a joyless existence, obeying all the 'Christian rules', like avoiding smoking, drinking, sex, laughter, fashion, cosmetics and only daring to breathe on alternate Thursday afternoons. They have been taught badly, and the Devil is only too delighted.

Some young people are like this too, struggling to behave as well as they can, and yet knowing that, deep down, they are not sure if it's worth it. They are in a sad netherland between glory and misery — they cannot rejoice in their salvation, because they are unsure of it, and they cannot revel in sin, because they know it's wrong. Their minds are full of truth, but it has not become reality for them in their hearts. They tend to give the right answer, but they don't really believe it themselves.

They are like the little boy in Sunday School who looked puzzled when the vicar asked the class, 'What do we call the little furry red or grey animal with a bushy tail, who runs along the branches of the trees, storing nuts for the winter?' and answered, 'Well, it sounds like a squirrel, but I think the answer should be Jesus.' His head told him one thing, while in his heart of hearts, he knew differently. Perhaps they once (or many times) gave their heart to Jesus, and became a Christian, but no one ever helped them to be sure that they were saved.

The threat of punishment hangs over them, and they know they deserve it. They are absolutely convicted of their sinfulness; they have certainly not been perfect since the day they went forward, or 'prayed a prayer', and they believe they may still be sent to hell when they die; so, in the meantime, they might as well practise.

Helping young people overcome a lack of assurance seems to be a neglected skill, but one which is easily acquired. I have spoken to a number of young people, and shown them a few Scriptures about themselves. The Word of God is living and active, and contains the remedy for this wasting disease.

*Therefore, there is now no condemnation for those who are in Christ Jesus ... For I am convinced that neither death nor life, neither angels nor demons, neither the present nor the future, nor any powers, neither height nor depth, nor anything else in all creation, will be able to separate us from the love of God that is in Christ Jesus our Lord* (Rom. 8:1,38,39).

Explain that they are in Christ Jesus if they have become a Christian. Ask if they can remember a definite time when they became a Christian, or if there is any evidence of them having been saved. Ask them if their parents or friends have ever accused them of being a Christian. Help them to see that their temporary worry or fear does not disqualify them from the benefits of the work Christ did for them at Calvary.

If God has declared them worthy because He chose to save them and adopt them into His family, who are they to dispute the fact? This, surely, is arrogance, to say that I know better than God! Let's train our young people to be full of joy about their salvation, and not to be anxious or to live in fear.

# Baptism in the Holy Spirit

This is vital, and available for every Christian. I am sure that God wants us to live in the fullness He has made available. Let's pray with the young people, and invite God's Spirit to fill them so that they may exercise spiritual gifts, know His power, and sense His presence filling every part of their lives.

For me, this took place twelve years after I was saved, but it would be infinitely preferable if it were twelve minutes afterwards (some might even be happy if it was twelve milliseconds). We want to be obedient to the Scripture:

*Do not get drunk on wine, which leads to debauchery. Instead, be filled with the Spirit* (Eph. 5:18).

This Scripture speaks of a constantly repeated filling of the Holy Spirit (the verb form is one which means 'be being filled'). We need not just the initial baptism of the Holy Spirit, but also a constant, daily refilling with His power and gifting.

Let's be careful that we teach the young people with accuracy. The baptism in the Spirit is not so that we can 'bring words' (an unhelpfully sloppy shorthand for the sharing of prophetic or instructive insights) to gain cred with our friends; it is so that we might be empowered by God to live lives which please Him and which declare His grace to a needy world.

While nothing should be done in a corner, or deliberately hidden away from view, praying for young people for baptism in the Spirit is not a 'spectator ministry'; take those who have responded to one side of the room, and encourage the others to pray, or to continue in worship. Alternatively, close the meeting.

One of the most important things to do is to discover if the young person has responded to a message, or felt a need, or if they genuinely desire the baptism of the Holy Spirit. Are they eager to be filled with power to serve God? Have they understood the implications of the baptism of the Spirit? I am not sure that every 'i' must be dotted and every 't' crossed as we explain the activity of the Holy Spirit, but it is good to be clear. Asking the young person why they want to be baptised in the Holy Spirit may isolate any areas of misunderstanding; as you chat through the issues, they may reveal other areas of ignorance, fear or need.

When you have assessed the situation, constantly asking God to give you insight and wisdom, then you should explain what you intend to do. You may feel they are not ready, and you might want to ask them to give the issues more thought — recommend that they read John 7:25–44 again, for example. Perhaps the person before you is a 'responder' — they invariably go forward or raise their hand at the slightest provocation, possibly due to insecurity, or a desire for attention. But in many cases, you will feel willing to pray for them to be baptised in the Holy Spirit.

Tell them that you will lay hands on them (if you're going to), so that it won't come as a surprise. Ask them to be open to God and to pray with you. Tell them that this is about participation, and not just a matter of letting God do something to you. He wants to work with them in gifting them, empowering them for witnessing, ministry and worship. Tell them that they may find themselves wanting to praise God, and that they should feel free to do so.

Then, simply invite God to baptise them with the Holy Spirit. Don't prolong the prayer time, or get worked up into a lather, as this is often more of a hindrance than a help. Stop after a couple of minutes, and ask them what is happening. If nothing, then continue.

If something is happening, but the young person cannot verbalise it, then continue. If they are able to be specific, then focus on that and continue in prayer. Be open to God revealing things to you.

Pray with faith, but be careful not to put any pressure on the young people to perform, or to speak in tongues immediately. The New Testament incidents of baptism of the Spirit show that different people had different experiences. My testimony is that I suddenly found myself speaking in tongues during a prayer time.

I have prayed with many young people for baptism in the Spirit, and in a good many cases found that they have been released into this particular gift during a subsequent worship time, as God gave them freedom. This is, I feel, preferable to protracted sessions of intense pressure, where the young person is tempted to fake it just to please the person who is praying for them. This encourages no one, and is not honouring towards God.

The baptism of the Holy Spirit is received by faith, and therefore it is not always the case that there are obvious physical signs that this has taken place.

We are not even guaranteed that we will feel tingles or goose bumps.

Take God at His Word, that He has sent the Spirit to empower and fill us, and invite the young person to trust God, step out in faith and be ready and willing to serve and honour God with his or her life. The work of God will be shown in the fruit of the life of each believer.

# Fruit

*By their fruit you will recognise them. Do people pick grapes from thornbushes, or figs from thistles? Likewise every good tree bears good fruit, but a bad tree bears bad fruit. A good tree cannot bear bad fruit, and a bad tree cannot bear good fruit* (Matt. 7:16–18).

The only real evidence of new life within a person is the fruit of the Spirit. If the spirit of Jesus is living within us, then we will exhibit some of His characteristics; perhaps not in full measure, but increasingly, as we grow in Him and become more and more like Him.

Young people need to know that there is hope for their lives. Many are overwhelmed by the apparently endless demands on them to live holy lives. Others are very aware of weaknesses in their character, and give up. But this verse and the context of the passage in Galatians 5 which describes the fruit of the Spirit promises that these characteristics are part of us; they are integral to our new identity as the sons and daughters of God. We must teach young people that they are (to continue with Jesus' imagery of plant life) no longer thistles; they are now fig trees, and they will produce good fruit, since God, the source of the Christian lives, is good. Obviously there is a measure of co-operation needed here, and we each have a responsibility to increase the crop of fruit. Refer again to Philippians 3:12–14.

A friend of mine became a Christian in his early teens, but after a while, he allowed his commitment to weaken, and he became a backslider. However, even while he was living a life which was far from 'Christian', one of his friends noticed that there was something different, something 'spiritual' about him. He has since returned to full commitment to the Lord, and he told me that he realises that even while he was in a backslidden state, the Spirit of God within him was still producing fruit. He had become, by new birth, a fig tree, as it were, and even though he was living the life of a thistle, he was still producing figs — even though they were weak, tasteless, small, and looked, to the casual observer, a lot like donkey food.

There is hope for the backslider, but let's be careful to help young people to produce quality, God-honouring fruit.

# Gifts

God chooses to give good gifts to His children, and young people are no exception. Theirs is not a junior version of the Holy Spirit — they get the full works, just like adults! It is extraordinary to observe young people exercising the gifts God has given them. I have been in meetings where God speaks powerfully through young people's prophetic insights, and where adults break down in conviction and repentance before a Holy God.

Let's be ready to encourage young people as they share their pictures or words of knowledge or wisdom; let's be ready to be sensitive to the timing of these words and the power with which they are being shared.

I have developed a policy of asking the young people to invite God to speak to them, and when He does, to ask Him if the message is for them or for everyone, and if it is for everyone, when should they share it. When they feel they have something to share, they come forward and speak to one of the team (not the worship leader, because that individual is busy leading the worship), and thus it is possible for the youth worker to make sure that what they are about to share is sound doctrinally, appropriate for everyone to hear, correctly timed, and as complete as possible.

It is helpful to ask young people to clarify the interpretation of the picture they want to share. There is the famous story about the person who shared a bizarre, mind-boggling picture of a penguin on a tightrope and yet had absolutely no idea of what the imagery signified — the meaning is the most important element, and if the interpretation is unclear or not given, then the body of Christ is bewildered, when God intended us to be edified.

I ask young people to stretch their faith to the limits. In one case, a young man came and spoke to a team member about someone who was being a bully at school, and getting into trouble. When he stepped up to the microphone and shared this, no one responded. So the young man was challenged to ask God for more details, and he was soon announcing that it was a male, and that he was sitting in the third row, over towards the coffee-bar side of the meeting room. He knew exactly who it was, since God had revealed it to him, but it would have been unwise for him to have mentioned names. I made it clear that God wasn't intending to condemn anyone, but to bring conviction, so that the person who was bullying could be set free from it, because he wasn't enjoying it and wanted to stop.

When the bully identified himself, the person who had been sharing the word of knowledge and a team member went to pray privately with him, and he repented of his sin, and when he had opportunity, made restitution with those he had been bullying. I believe that he may not have responded until he knew that God was fully aware of the details, and that He wasn't going to come down heavy on him, but provide a way of escape from his behaviour pattern.

God does not identify individuals or sins or attitudes in order to embarrass, ridicule or punish them, but He is motivated by love and a desire to put things right.

For a number of years I avoided responding to words of knowledge and specific revelations which certainly applied to me, because I was afraid of what others would think of me. I have since realised that I disqualified myself from receiving God's blessing, and from getting things sorted out, dealt with and changed. Therefore I am now eager to encourage young people to think highly of those who are responding, because it means that they are putting things right with God — confessing sins, changing attitudes, correcting behaviour. It is not the past which is important; it is the present, and the future. It is not what Saul of Tarsus used to be that mattered; once the sins were confessed, the attitudes were changed and the behaviour was corrected, the question that mattered became: what was the Apostle Paul going to do with his life?

I feel we need to encourage young people to exercise the gifts of the Holy Spirit, but without placing an unhelpful over-emphasis on them. Christian character, knowledge of the Bible, a healthy prayer life, a diligence in evangelism, financial generosity, righteous speech, control over sinful passions; all of these are just as important, as they are all elements of God's plan for our lives.

# Teaching on basic doctrines

I was teaching a group of young people about the cross, when I thought I'd just try a little experiment. I asked them what 'substitutionary atonement' was. No one knew, but one witty lad asked, 'Is it a Greek island?'

There is little benefit in training teenagers to grapple with long words, theological expressions and doctrinal phrases, such as the hypostatic union, soteriology or pneumatology. As I've often said, if you don't know what eschatology is, it's not the end of the world.

The point is that while young people certainly need to know about these great doctrines, they will resist learning long words or anything which sounds off-putting. This is not an anti-intellectual stance, but simply good sense. Let's generate excitement about the fact that Jesus was fully God and fully man, encouraging the young people to worship a Saviour who laid aside His majesty, took on human form, is able to understand all our suffering and weaknesses because He experienced them, and yet remained sinless so that His death on the cross was able to save us from the punishment we deserve. It would be a disaster if the teenagers were put off learning such powerful and vital truths by a poor presentation or a Bible College type of approach.

I believe it is worthwhile teaching a wide range of biblical doctrines: creation, redemption, atonement, salvation, the person and work of the Holy Spirit, the cross, the resurrection, the return of Christ, grace, the ultimate value of good works, praise, worship, healing, doctrine of the church, prayer and many more. But these have not been taught in strict succession, or in isolation from practical aspects of the teaching programme, such as how to witness to your friends at school, how to spend time alone with God, attitude to parents, making and keeping friendships, the urge to merge (dating), walking consistently with God, and so on. In addition, other teaching has helped young people to trust God, to expand their faith and to give them vision for personal and corporate growth. There is a need for prophetic teaching and for interpreting the times as well. For example, Joshua's position as the successor to Moses has lessons for those who are the sons and daughters of those who have pioneered in the renewal and restoration of the church.

# Group prayer

Learning how to pray together is an important part of the Christian life. I am glad I was thrown in at the deep end soon after I was converted, and learned to pray aloud in a group setting. This helped my confidence, and, once I was through a phase of trying to sound impressive, it helped me to be able to express myself to the Lord in front of others.

These days there is, in some circles, a helpful trend towards everyone raising their voices together with one accord, and filling the room with sound. This is great for the less confident, who might never pray aloud if they thought anyone could hear them.

When I pray with small groups of young people, they tend to jockey for position, and all pray once. They don't seem to mind praying something that someone else has already prayed (perhaps because I teach them to be persistent in prayer, and to be full of faith and keep on asking until they have received that for which they are asking).

Let's please be careful not to raise up another generation of people who pray 'Lord, Lord' or 'just really' prayers. I was once in a meeting where the subject of the talk was the Lordship of Christ. Someone closed the meeting by asking God to help us ' ... to just really be in charge of our lives, that you, Lord, might be lord, Lord ... ' or some such expression. The way the prayer was phrased made it amusing rather than earnest. When we speak naturally to one another, we do not keep on using each other's names in every sentence, and when we cannot think of what we want to say, we use a much simpler technique. Most of us say 'er' or 'um'. Why can't we do that when we're praying?

And let's be a bit more thoughtful about the grunting which indicates agreement. Let's be ready to agree with someone when they make a good point in prayer, and we could even do that by saying something truly creative, like 'Yes, Lord' or 'That's right' instead of making farmyard noises, which so often punctuate our prayer meetings — we might as well do sea-lion impressions, just to ring the changes.

On another occasion, I was in a bizarre prayer meeting where some English-speakers and some Portuguese-speakers were together for prayer. One of the Portuguese men was praying loudly and with some passion, in Portuguese. I have to admit that I got a bit bored, so I started to grunt in time with his phrases, not having the slightest clue of what he was going on about, but wanting to feel as if I was taking part in the meeting. The other English-speakers were amused, but we all joined in when he reached 'Amen', which we did understand.

By the way, do you know the two words which are universal — everyone knows both of them, in every language in the world? They are 'Hallelujah' and 'Coca-Cola'. So if you ever find yourself in Namibia, or Peru, or even Western Samoa, you can publicly thank God when the fizzy drinks arrive.

Young people find it difficult and embarrassing to pray aloud, since this is not something which comes naturally to them. We need to help them overcome their natural disinclinations, to take a step of faith and to pray. God loves to hear His children speaking to Him, expressing their love for Him and their dependence on Him, and He loves to answer our prayers, as well!

It is important to give systematic teaching on prayer — the need for faith, righteousness and specific requests, the need to pray within the will of God, the power of the name of Jesus, and the spiritual warfare we can enter as we pray.

As I and other members of the team have done this, I have been very pleased to see a great increase in the amount and the quality of the prayers the young people spontaneously offer up to God during the worship times, at the prayer meetings, and when they are in small groups.

# Healing prayer

I have witnessed instant healings too often to ever deny that God heals in this way, but I would not claim that He does so every time. Sometimes, healing is partial; sometimes it is gradual; sometimes, for His own good reasons, God chooses not to heal.

I have prayed diligently for two friends who have, sadly, died from cancer, and I have prayed with very little faith and very briefly for some teenagers with severe skin complaints, and seen it disappear before my eyes. The young people once prayed briefly with an adult visitor to the church, and heard later that his injured leg had been made completely well in a couple of weeks, where it had taken six months to improve hardly at all, despite medical attention and physiotherapy.

God is in control; He is the creator of the human body and He is able to heal any illness, injury or abuse. He is also Lord, and His will is always right and true. My two friends who died are now with Him in a better place, and I cannot say that God was cruel to bless them with release from pain and disability. Yet I have to ask 'why?' People can survive skin complaints, yet they are healed instantly. Others are eaten up from the inside by cancer, and they die. God knows.

This is at the front of my mind when training the young people to pray for one another to be well. I want to encourage them to be full of faith, and to trust God for the outcome. It's up to Him. My own faith levels are greatly increased when God gives someone a word of knowledge about His intention to heal a specific illness, injury or abuse. In such a case, I will be prepared to extend the prayer time a little longer. It is tremendous to be around when someone is healed, and young people witness it. They get so excited about their God and His amazing power!

Let's be bold to take God at His Word and to pray for people to be set free, delivered, healed and restored. And let's leave the results to Him and His higher wisdom.

It is unhelpful to have too many young people crowding round 'the sick one', and it is downright unpleasant sometimes. For example, I knew a young man with verrucas (nasty warts on his feet). For a few weeks, young people would gather round him at the end of the meeting and pray for the verrucas to be healed, and the young man often removed his shoes and socks, so that the evidence could be witnessed. After an hour's football, his feet were not the most sweet-smelling, and the room was filled with a stench. I was glad when God healed him, for many reasons! Ultimately, I feel that our approach could have been wiser, and that I might have asked that the praying be done in a more orderly way, and with greater awareness of the genuine danger of infection from his feet to the skin of those praying for him. I am not lacking in faith, just trying to be practical.

The regular visits to this country of John Wimber and his teams have given us the encouragement and some guidelines in praying for healing; get a general description of the symptoms before you start — not a complete medical history, but some idea of what the problem is. Check for unconfessed sin, bitterness, wrong motives, etc., asking the Holy Spirit to reveal to you anything which might be the root of the illness or disease. Pray to God, not to the sickness, and pray in the name of Jesus. Avoid excessive or inappropriate laying-on of hands, and, in general, avoid mixed-gender groups. Don't forget to thank God when He heals the sick person, and wait a little while, in case God wants to give anyone an instruction or insight into avoiding the recurrence of the problem.

# Counsel

The pastor-heart within me beats with uncertain regularity; I do not believe that I am particularly gifted in this area. I know that there has to be an element of pastoral awareness in order to teach on relevant subjects, but counselling young people with problems is a different matter altogether.

God is completely amazing, and He does cause massive, total, instant change in some people's lives at a stroke. We must be careful never to deny this — if in doubt, read Paul's account of his conversion once again (Acts 22:2–21). But more often, God will use a word of knowledge or a teaching point in a talk to trigger repentance or acknowledgement of a difficulty and it is then up to those with pastoral gifts and responsibility to lead the teenager through to repentance, faith, a change of attitude, deliverance or healing.

I have met many youth workers who possess great skill and sensitivity and who can help young people as they weep over their sin, receive forgiveness and change their minds about committing the same sins again. Others are gifted in confronting problems, or in gently understanding issues which are often very complex, and, due often to the immaturity of the person involved, incompletely expressed. I quickly become frustrated when I don't hear the whole story in a nut-shell; the pastorally-gifted cope magnificently, and gradually get to grips with the details.

But there is great joy in having young people respond to you in a pastoral setting. I share this with you because I am rather chuffed about it.

At a Bible Week, I saw Darren, one of our lads, holding the hand of a good-looking girl, and they were obviously enjoying one another's company. When I saw him alone a little later, I came on strong. 'Who is that girl?' He told me her name — Kate. 'When did she become a Christian?' I asked. 'Is she going on with God? When was she baptised in the Spirit? And if you don't know the answers, then why are you even *thinking* of becoming emotionally involved with her, eh?' He was a little taken aback, but realised that I was being very direct because I care about his walk with God, and didn't want him to be distracted by this beauty with her waving titian locks tumbling happily over her shoulders.

I was sitting in my tent the next morning, reading a book, when this girl stood in the entrance. I didn't immediately recognise her as Darren's friend. 'My name is Kate,' she announced, 'and I became a Christian when I was four. God baptised me with the Holy Spirit in 1986, and I first spoke in tongues during the *More than Conquerors* holiday. I am going on with God, and I am not about to lead Darren astray. Does that satisfy you?'

By this time I was chortling away, realising that my strong questions were being answered just as strongly. But I was delighted that Darren had chosen to befriend a girl of such quality, and that she was sufficiently secure to lay into me in this way, albeit respectfully. I had no hesitation in letting Darren know that I was very impressed and that, as his youth leader, approved of his choice of girlfriend.

*And we urge you, brethren, admonish the unruly, encourage the fainthearted, help the weak, be patient with all men* (1 Thess 5:14, NASB).

This is a key verse, instructing us in pastoral care, and it is much more forthright in the New American Standard Bible, so that's what I have used. It is important that we do not make the mistake of encouraging the unruly; they need stronger treatment, while the weak will be demoralised if we admonish them. We need to have a correct understanding of those in our care before we begin to deal with them, or we will perhaps fall into these kinds of error. Only God can give us this discernment, so let us pray for His help as we lead His people.

Much of the pastoral work of the youth group takes place during the meetings; that is, young people are convicted or challenged by the presence of God in the worship, or by a specific word of knowledge or insight. Others just have problems, and they choose to identify themselves during the meeting. In order to remove a potential distraction from the middle of the crowd, and to give a measure of privacy, it is appropriate to take them out of the meeting for a few minutes to chat and pray together.

On balance, I suppose this is fair enough, but sometimes I wonder if more good would be done by allowing the young person involved to hear the message which is being shared in the meeting, rather than sitting in the corridor or a counselling armchair.

> *For the word of God is living and active. Sharper than any double-edged sword, it penetrates even to dividing soul and spirit, joints and marrow; it judges the thoughts and attitudes of the heart* (Heb. 4:12).

Obviously, the counsellor is sharing Scriptures and speaking Bible truth into the situation; but there is a spiritual power in the preached Word which can be extremely effective. Ten minutes in personal conversation is probably all that can be usefully achieved while the meeting continues, and then it's time to get back to hear the speaker. Most counselling times seem more effective if they are short and to the point, in my view. Clearly, where there are deep-rooted issues which cannot be adequately handled by the team member, these are referred to the leadership team and then to elders, as appropriate.

The fact of the matter is that child abuse is on the increase;

we are beginning to hear young people share fearsome stories of what is happening to them. In such cases, it is vital that we do not promise complete confidentiality; in order to stop the offences happening, someone must be told. Specialists such as lawyers and social workers trained in handling such distressing cases need to be brought in at the very earliest opportunity.

The variety and breadth of counselling is too much for me to be able to give much help here; but God gives good gifts to His people, so that they can edify and encourage one another. Let's make ourselves available to young people, so that they know we are approachable, even if we may not have all the answers at our fingertips.

# Chapter Seven

# Issues Faced
# by Today's Teenagers

This will be a brief excursion through some of the concerns of young people, by way of a reminder, rather than a weighty discourse to inform or pontificate.

## Sexual pressure

No generation has ever faced such a weight of sexual pressure. Even those growing up in the '60s (such as ourselves, possibly), with all the intimidation and temptation of the permissive society, were not confronted on such a regular basis with overwhelming amounts of sexual imagery and innuendo.

The sweet innocence of Mary Hopkin ('Those Were the Days') has been replaced by the blatant sexuality of such people as Madonna, Michael Jackson and Prince.

Advertisers are increasingly using nudity and sexually provocative images. Products with little or no sexual connotations are nevertheless placed in a context which says, 'If you buy this, you'll be more successful with the opposite sex.'

The condom culture has led to an advert in a teen magazine which said, 'It used to be that sex was for marriage. But now that's changed.' Condom manufacturers in America are no longer allowed to refer to 'safe sex'. They have to call it 'safer sex', since the number of sexually transmitted diseases has increased, and the performance of condoms in preventing the exchange of body fluids has been proven to be far less than reliable.

Are we providing young people with reasons for our stand against premarital sexual activity? Why should they wait? Let's be ready with positive answers. I believe there are four main reasons.

- *Physical reasons:* sin against your own body; sexually transmitted diseases; unwanted pregnancy and abortion; to preserve the giving nature and beauty of marital sex.
- *Spiritual reasons:* avoid judgement; walk in holiness; be a positive influence; exercise patience; waiting builds trust; Jesus can fill the void.
- *Emotional reasons:* avoid being compared with previous partners; guilt; it's hard to break up; destruction of self-esteem; waiting demonstrates maturity and respect; be dignified; only one first time.
- *Relationship reasons:* sex can become dominant, more important than love; sex is special — for marriage relationship only.

What about lesbian and gay issues? Do we help young people make up their minds on this? Are we standing back, and letting the world promote its message of 'If it feels good, do it!' without restraint? Or are we simply being judgemental and dismissive?

It is vital that we have answers, since the questions are certainly being asked. There is a school sex-education video currently being used in London and elsewhere which shows a couple preparing for sex, and the only advice given is 'use a condom'! The next scene shows two boys making the same preparations, and they are given the same advice. A third scene features two girls. Is this really the best the educationalist can do — provide a sheath and make no moral judgements at all?

My own view is that this sort of education actively encourages immorality and a blurring of the gender-boundaries, at the very least. It's okay to be gay. Or is it? No it isn't!

There are some learned people who will dismiss Leviticus 18:22, but I would ask them to note the immediate context — verse 21 is about child-sacrifice, and verse 23 mentions bestiality. God clearly abominates homosexual acts. He has a holy hatred of their sin. Let's not compromise by being slow to condemn sin as sin.

But don't forget that God loves the sinner, and that we can draw on His reserves of grace to show understanding and compassion to those who are sinning in this way.

# Peer pressure

Teenagers are very prone to following the herd. Even when they know the facts, they will be loathe to disagree with others, especially when they have to be the odd one out.

There was once a famous psychology experiment conducted using a dozen teenagers in a classroom. Eleven of them were briefed to give the same wrong answer to a question, and the twelfth person was not. The class was then asked to do some additions in their heads, and the young people were asked to raise their hands when the correct answer was mentioned by the teacher.

A number of sums were performed, and then the class was asked to add fifteen and six in their heads. Possible answers were suggested. 'Nineteen.' No one moved. 'Twenty-three.' Not a flinch. 'Twenty-two.' Eleven hands shot confidently into the air. The only dissenter was the person who had not been briefed, but after a few seconds, he too raised his hand in acknowledgement that fifteen plus six makes twenty-two. The experiment was repeated with several groups of young people, and in every case, no one wanted to be the odd one out. That's the power of peer pressure!

Perhaps it is fear of being proved wrong, but there is certainly something which drives young people particularly to want to be accepted by the rest of the crowd, and to be prepared to claim to believe something they know to be untrue, just to keep the peace.

Going against the flow is hard for us all, but when you add the insecurity of being a teenager to the natural tendency to want to be in accord with everyone else, then the likelihood of a young person being prepared to stand up and be counted as a Christian is slim indeed.

Young Christians have a particularly difficult time, since the enemy of souls is out to get them, too! Let's be determined to help them by examining the character of Jesus, and giving guidelines on how to be different, avoiding places where temptations are strong, etc. Young people are often prepared to testify to occasions when they have faced opposition, and been in a 'lion's den', so to speak, and this is of great encouragement to others.

Jesus' words compare well with Paul's:

*But when they arrest you, do not worry about what to say or how to say it. At that time you will be given what to say, for it will not be you speaking, but the Spirit of your Father speaking through you* (Matt. 10:19,20).

*... Always be prepared to give an answer to everyone who asks you to give the reason for the hope that you have. But do this with gentleness and respect ...* (1 Pet. 3:15).

If we arm our young people with a prepared answer, or at least a good idea of the gist of what they want to communicate, then they can truly rely on the Holy Spirit to give them the precise words to say when they are faced with situations which call upon them to stand up and be counted.

# Rebellion against parental authority

Many parents do a great job of trying to understand their teenagers, and the changes that are happening to their relationship with them. Nevertheless, some teenagers feel very trapped, even when their parents do well. The natural rebellion is fuelled by media images of alienation and defiance. The sinful nature is hard at work in young people.

I was converted early in my teenage years, and my parents did their best to allow me to grow towards adulthood. But even then there were difficulties — understanding one another was practically impossible; we had theological differences; my schoolwork was a constant source of contention ... My point is that Christian families are not immune from trials and troubles as young people grow up into adulthood.

Young people are surrounded with rules and laws, and they want to break free. While it is right and proper that they should break free of some of the more child-protective rules of the home (tie your money in the corner of your hanky; come straight home from school; finish your broccoli), it is inappropriate for them to rebel against laws of the land and the school rules which still apply to them.

Haircuts can be a source of constant irritation; if the

parents impose 'sensible' ones, then many young people will find this annoying; but if the young people are allowed to have whatever trendy style they prefer, then doubtless some parents will find it difficult to remain even-tempered! Clothes, music, cosmetics, coming-home times, sibling rivalry, diction ... There seems to be no end to the number of things teenagers can do wrong, in the eyes of their parents. Similarly, teenagers are often impossible to please; parents do their best to understand them, and they are rewarded with accusations of interference.

One young person said to me, 'If I stay in my room and listen to records, I get told to come down and behave like a member of the family; and if I do, I get criticised for my manners or my hair or my clothes or the way I speak. I can't win!' When all family members obey the Word of God, there will be a distinct increase in the level of domestic unity.

> *Children, obey your parents in everything, for this pleases the Lord. Fathers, do not embitter your children, or they will become discouraged* (Col. 3:20,21).

Perhaps young people feel that they are not children any more. Fair enough. But they still need to obey the Word of God.

> *If it is possible, as far as it depends on you, live at peace with everyone* (Rom. 12:18).

Gotcha! But there must be room for some compromise and discussion as teenagers begin to become adults. This is no excuse, however, for rebellion and disharmony in the home, particularly if it is a Christian home.

Someone once remarked that parents are the kind of people least suited to looking after children and teenagers. But the fact remains that young people are the responsibility of the parents, and the youth group is supposed to be a place to add to the teaching they are receiving at home, backing parents up, and to give an opportunity for young people to interact with their peers in a safe environment. The reality seems to be that there is not a great deal of teaching given by parents to teenagers, in many cases, and that the attitude which prevails among teenagers is that parents are wrong, old-fashioned and deliberately obstructive.

However, let's be positive. I know a family where the sons are given bunk-notes from school so that they can be taken by their father to rock concerts. The father (who is a parent governor of the school) claims that these concerts are important elements in his son's musical education. His sons love and respect him, acknowledging his faults, but grateful for his relaxed attitude towards double geography. The sons do well in their exams, by the way. Especially geography.

I know some people will find this approach a little too relaxed, but at least the parent here is attempting to communicate acceptance and respect for his sons' musical tastes and is showing a genuine interest in them.

## Finances

Pocket money is almost a thing of the past. Most young people want the right to earn as much cash as they can, and to spend it all on luxury items, such as music, hi-fi's, fashionable clothes, junk food, entertainment (shows, concerts, films) and cosmetics.

Their entire income is disposable; the thought of giving to God's work, or of spending any of their income on such mundane things as housekeeping, their share of the TV licence, or the electricity bill does not occur to them.

We need to be careful to help young people to choose their jobs carefully. Some I have known have burdened themselves with horrendous amounts of work, simply for the money; two morning paper rounds, stocking shelves in a shop after school, then an evening paper round, followed by homework. And all day Saturday working in a grocer's store. Little wonder they are wealthy — they don't have time to spend it! They are exhausting themselves at great cost to their schoolwork, and to their social life. We need to be able to speak into this, and give appropriate counsel, as long as we do not go against parental wishes.

Teaching young people to have an open-handed approach towards money is vital. Are they giving any of their cash to the church? What about getting into debt? Are they saving any? Are they displaying greed or generosity? All of these are vital lessons to learn in this increasingly materialistic society.

## Educational expectations

When I was at school, there were enormous pressures put on me to go to university and to study for what seemed to me to be the rest of my life. Would I ever be free of exams? More to the point, would I ever be free of revision, or of exam results? I dealt with these pressures in the best way I knew how — by failing my A levels!

But surely we have a more practical (and Godly) attitude towards our lives and the direction we wish to take. Young people need to know not only the importance of planning ahead and doing the best they possibly can, but about the important things in life, too. Do they want to study? Could they cope with living in a pressure-cooker environment for three more years? Are they better served by taking some more practical training, or a shorter course of study?

Some of the females will have set their sights on marriage as the goal of their lives, and they will perhaps need to be persuaded to consider something else, just in case Mr Right doesn't come along straight away. And even if he does, there are plenty of alternatives to becoming a housewife and mother while still a teenager.

Obviously, parents need to help their offspring in finding the right level and amount of work they should be doing, but we can help in giving good advice, making sure that at least club night is a time when they can relax and be themselves. This is just one of the reasons why it is important to ensure that our teaching times do not emulate school; the young people come partly to escape that, and we should be sensitive to this.

## Forming habits

Nearly every teenager satisfies their curiosity about tobacco in some secluded place (behind the bike sheds, or in a wood), armed with a packet of five Park Drive or, if money's no object, ten Woodbines, and a box of Swan. Yes, you're right, this is indeed personal testimony. After some spluttering, and considerable disappointment at what the adverts call *flavour* turning out to be nothing but choking fumes, they will either give up, or persevere.

There is a lot of talk about passive smoking being bad for the lungs, but the worst part, it seems to me, is the strong image implanted by being in the company of adults who smoke. I will say it firmly: youth leaders should not be smokers. Lighting up in front of the young people is a lousy example to set — you are in bondage to the habit, which makes you a poor role-model — and sneaking off afterwards for a quick drag out of sight brands you as deceptive and hypocritical. And don't think, as I did for many years, that no one knows. The smell gets everywhere, and no amount of extra strong mints can adequately cover up.

When young people take up smoking as a habit, they are either rebelling or trying to behave as adults. Experiments are finished with; this is a decision. The issue of polluting your body with toxic fumes and chemicals should be addressed head-on, long before the habits can be formed. My testimony is that the habit is almost impossible to break, but that the grace of God is sufficient, if it's mixed with a strong desire to quit and a good group of non-smoking friends to encourage you.

Alcohol is exciting, too, giving young people the thrill of being like an adult, without any of the responsibilities. It is my belief that youth leaders need not abstain totally from alcohol, since they can be a role-model in some circumstances, proving that to drink only a moderate amount demonstrates self-control. This is weakish argument, since the young people are not allowed in the pub to watch you drink your pint or two. But there is value in communicating that you are walking in obedience to the biblical injunction to refrain from drunkenness. Moderate drinking differs from moderate smoking since an occasional drink is good for you, while tobacco smoke only harms, in small or large quantities.

Other drugs, such as so-called soft drugs (hash, joints, spliffs, etc.) or hard drugs (XTC, crack, smack, H, snow, cocaine) are widely available. How can we educate this generation to avoid getting involved? 'Just say No!' isn't enough. Why say 'No'?

There are tell-tale signs which can help you recognise young people who are using restricted substances: glazed eyes; uncharacteristic disinterest in things; a new-found poverty; fresh sores; changes in personality and appearance; aggression when questioned. Speak to their friends; they will know. I think it is our responsibility to inform parents, and it is up to parents to decide about involving the police. But consider what you will do if you discover that someone is in possession of illegal drugs while they are on church premises.

I was astonished to read somewhere that there are now several rehabilitation clinics in New York and other major cities in the States for young adults who have become hooked on video games. Mario is more widely recognised among American children than Mickey Mouse. The meteoric rise in popularity achieved by video games is of some concern, because there are few things better designed to waste time and money. Having your name on the top ten scoreboard represents hours and hours of expensive practice.

Of course, there is great fun to be had in an amusement arcade or from Nintendo or Lynx games systems, and most people come to no harm. But there are some youngsters who cannot set a time limit, or who expect to spend a sizeable amount of money when they play.

I have taken a crowd of teens to the local pier, and played with them on video games, but I made sure that they knew I had set myself a time limit of an hour and a cash limit of £2.50 and that I expected them to set their own limits; this meant we had to be very selective about what we played and how often, since our cash soon ran out. I reckon I got my money's worth, and showed them how to beat the system.

Other young people play the fruit machines, and, while it seems that some win a little, most lose a lot. Let's inform our young people that the machines are designed to make money for the owners, and that they only pay out a proportion of what is put in. And it's expensive entertainment, watching those bells and plums whizz round, as the gambling bug begins to bite.

Why do young people experiment with such things, when they know before they start that they might not be able to stop? Perhaps part of it is that they think that to drink or to puff joints will make them more of an adult. To a certain extent that's true, but it is our desire to teach them that they are accepted as they are, that to pretend to be something you're not is foolish, and that to achieve so-called 'adulthood' by committing yourself to some leech-like habit is a pretty feeble achievement. Let's be diligent in giving them so many great reasons to avoid these habits, that they will hear us and walk free of them.

*Do not let sin reign in your mortal body so that you obey its evil desires* (Rom. 6:12).

# The occult

There is great interest in the unknown, and young people are naturally curious. The New Age movement has been built on the inquisitive nature of people when it comes to mystical and hidden things.

Perhaps interest begins with reading your stars in the paper. School friends may have tarot cards or ouija boards, and curiosity is not yet satisfied. It's not far from there until Dennis Wheatley novels, many of the Hammer films and actual occult practices begin to exercise their grip on young people's minds and imaginations.

The enemy is delighted when we begin to dabble. He is not concerned with teaching us the reality about evil; he is happy just to keep our curiosity alive. In direct contrast, Jesus is the Truth. When we find Him, we discover all we need to know. Our interest becomes commitment and love, not a downward spiral into the unknown.

What can we do, as youth leaders, to help the teenagers in our care to avoid these dangers? Perhaps clear teaching on the difference between the kingdom of light and the kingdom of darkness would be a good start. Frank explanations of how the astrological predictions are compiled (not all astrologers are charlatans — some are occult masters); an investigation into what can make palmistry, ouija boards and tarot readings accurate; the dangers of so-called 'white' magic, and so on.

Someone said that we can fall into two equal and opposite errors: either we pay too little attention to the enemy, or too much. If we paid a little bit more attention to his ways, we might steal his thunder and give away some of the secrets before young people find out for themselves, and get into sinful or ensnared situations.

Two practical issues: the danger of being enticed into the occult by such role-playing fantasy games as *Dungeons and Dragons* is probably not enormous, except in cases where the young people are playing the games at a high level consistently, where demons and wizards are often important characters in the story, and are therefore at the forefront of their minds.

Secondly, I had to stop and think hard when the video playing as background in the coffee bar at the youth group one night was a *Scooby-Doo* cartoon. Is it right for us to be showing this? Ghosts, ghoulies and things that go bump in the night have their roots in the occult. Such cartoons are a mild form of reinforcement of the values of the kingdom of darkness. It's up to you to make up your own mind. In the final analysis, *Scooby-Doo* is probably harmless, in comparison with the dreadful violence and anarchy of *Tom and Jerry*, or the anti-authority attitudes applauded by *Boss Cat*. Could I be writing this with tongue in cheek? Get into small groups and discuss.

# GIGO

The mnemonic GIGO was, I believe, invented by computer programmers, and it stands for Garbage In, Garbage Out. Clearly, if your programme or the data you feed into the computer is duff, the result will be unreliable or perhaps just plain wrong. The same goes for our minds.

The number of video nasties which are available grows every week; many are freely available for young people to rent or buy. As violent physical harm is done to humans and animals in front of our eyes (sometimes without using special effects), our sensitivity to seeing these things is reduced. If we let our minds dwell on images that corrupt or defile, we are disobeying scriptural injunction.

> *Finally, brothers, whatever is true, whatever is noble, whatever is right, whatever is pure, whatever is lovely, whatever is admirable — if anything is excellent or praiseworthy — think about such things* (Phil. 4:8).

Pornography is becoming increasingly offensive. When I was a lad, the copy of *Men Only* which circulated around the changing rooms showed topless models, with an occasional glimpse of derrière. I understand that such 'tame' stuff is not to be found any longer.

Intimacy is debased, and no amount of arguing about 'adult education' or 'harmless titillation' will convince me that it is 'all part of growing up'. Women are degraded enough in our society without allowing this sort of material to be circulated among those with impressionable minds. If young people fill their thoughts with these kinds of sexually provocative images, they will not be walking in holiness and Godliness.

GIGO also operates (although less obviously) with the Summer Romance novel. Some teenage girls give their spare time to books which feature manly characters with firm chins, barrel chests and overbearing or charming manners who meet, annoy and then woo slim blonde or red-headed beauties. Clearly, such stories can give teenagers false expectations and low self-esteem and give them unhelpful exposure to trashy writing styles.

How can we help young people to be discerning about how they fill their minds? Let's be bold in discussing films with young people, finding agreement on what is helpful, knowing how to judge what a film is going to be like from the publicity, etc. I believe that one of the key factors is to make sure that not only are we good role-models, but that we point our teenagers towards excellent marriages. If we influence teenagers positively, then their response will be similarly positive. GIGO can stand for Good In, Good Out, too!

Examine the lives of the disciples, and see how they learned from Jesus, doing the things He did, learning from His example.

# Sexism

We need to take care that we do not perpetuate inaccurate views and assumptions about the roles of the sexes, since young people these days will very quickly pick up on these and accuse us of sexism. The fact remains that we should respect our brothers and sisters as equals in Christ. Let each one serve according to his or her gift.

That is to say that a woman must not be put down as

someone who is only capable of making tea or washing up, and that a man must not be defined in terms of dominance, physical labour and a lack of artistic style. There is a thin line on which we must balance. To stereotype men as macho tough guys, and women as dainty weaklings, is both rude and inaccurate; it is equally sexist to picture women as dominant and overbearing or men as weak, hen-pecked wimps.

Most of all, we should listen carefully to Jesus' comment that leaders must be the servants of all (Matt. 20:26–28). Let's be prepared to let the pendulum swing towards having talented, gifted women teaching our young people, or leading worship, or exercising other gifts, while men take a back seat or get on with cleaning the toilets, for example.

# Racism

I am surprised at the number of times when young people make remarks which betray a poor attitude towards ethnic minorities. Racism is loathsome. There is no way people should be treated with disdain or dislike simply on account of the colour of their skin or their ancestry. It is certainly the case that people from different cultures have a different way of thinking, and therefore may need specialist treatment as we communicate the good news to them. But racism is hateful, and must be rebuked whenever it occurs.

Helping young people to gain a positive attitude towards ethnic minorities is perhaps best done by the slow, painful process of integration. Maintaining ignorance of one another is a recipe for maintaining prejudice; mixing up typical white middle-class English teenagers with others of a different hue or background can help to undermine any prejudices.

It has to be said that sometimes the hatred expressed towards minorities has resulted in those minorities becoming just as prejudiced against whites; this seems to me to be fair enough, but barrier-building, rather than bridge-building. Often our racial prejudice is mixed up with religious differences. Personally, I feel that I have little in common with Muslims, or Hindus; but I need to realise that I have little in common with atheists or people who live their lives in such a way as to deny the gospel and the love of God. I am not superior to any of these people; it is just that my sins have been forgiven; mercy has been shown to me. Religious differences also mean that there will be relatively few members of ethnic minorities in each Christian youth group; again the process of integration will take more time.

It is vital that we teach young people to welcome strangers and to treat them with kindness and friendship.

> *Do not forget to entertain strangers, for by so doing some people have entertained angels without knowing it* (Heb. 13:2).

## Persecution

There are many young people who are standing up for the Lord at school, and who are taking some stick for it. Teachers and other pupils alike can be hurtful in the way they treat Christians, mocking their beliefs, decrying their principles, deliberately putting stumbling blocks in their way, and rejoicing over any mistakes or minor slip-ups which may happen from time to time. This form of mental and social cruelty is very real for teenagers; it may not compare with prison or torture, which some Christians face, but it is nevertheless persecution.

Unbelievers can have a very high view of Christians, setting them on pedestals of integrity and sinless perfection. This, of course, requires that the Christian behaves not just in a way which is pure and righteous and holy, but that the Christian must act in a way which is pure and righteous and holy in the eyes of his human critics.

This is, I guarantee, impossible, because none of us can achieve the ludicrously high and inconsistent standards set by non-Christians. God, on the other hand, is full of love and mercy and compassion, and while He does not condone our sins and weaknesses, He is for us, not against us, and He is constantly on hand to help us, and He understands when we fall. He picks us up, forgives us through the blood of Jesus, and refills us with the Holy Spirit to help us to get it right on subsequent occasions. And God's standards are truly pure, and not motivated badly like the impossible standards of the Christian's critics.

Young people may have homework stolen or destroyed, bikes sabotaged, and countless occasions of name-calling for the sake of the gospel. Bullying is in a different league when everyone is ganging up on the 'weedy wet Christian', because it's easy to hide in the mob.

We must arm our young people with weapons to enable them to withstand the fiery darts of the evil one (often these come in the form of those who set themselves up as enemies at school), and to stand firm in the day of battle, and to win through, eventually.

*In fact, everyone who wants to live a godly life in Christ Jesus will be persecuted* (2 Tim. 3:12).

# Chapter Eight
# Variety in the Programme

The word most often on the lips of teenagers as they sneer at the opportunities placed before them is 'boring'. School is boring, TV is boring, having to finish their broccoli is boring, and, most of all, church is boring. The fact remains that none of these things are boring, except church (joke), but that they are predictable. School will be the same as last week. The TV shows will still pander to the lowest common denominator. Broccoli will always taste of broccoli (except when it's vindaloo broccoli, when it will taste of fire). Church is so often completely predictable too.

It is therefore one of our jobs as youth leaders to prevent our youth group events ever being described in this way. Every week at your youth group, give young people a chance to choose between a minimum of four activities, followed by a power hour where anything could happen! It is not predictable, except for the notices, which really are boring, even though the content is not.

One of the chief ways to combat predictability is to have a constant flow of new and fresh activities. Use resources such as the companion volume to this book *101 Dynamic Ideas for Your Youth Group*. Buy it today, folks! Put this book down right now, and go and buy it! I'll keep your place for you.

*      *      *

Welcome back! I hope you had a nice time at the local Christian bookshop. An unashamed plug, because I believe in the ideas contained in it, and I believe in the variety they may bring to tired youth leaders.

The key part is to make sure that the activities you offer each week balance. If football is on the list for tonight, then why not offer an alternative which requires a different set of skills

— like a Trivial Pursuit competition, or a speed chess tournament? If one activity focuses on the active body, then let another utilise the mind. If one is highly competitive, introduce an option which enhances the benefits of teamwork. Since the females are often harder to entice into events which demand active participation, then allow them to be involved in something more passive, like a panel game, or a Top of the Pops Workshop.

Are all your activities geared towards the males, since the females never join in anyway? Then organise a netball tournament, and give the girls every opportunity to win. Shout 'windmills', if you like. Do all your plans require social interaction? As a general rule, that is good, but now and again you could include something which is highly individual, like a fashion or painting workshop.

# Live a little!

Is everything always safe, tried and tested? Good. But once in a while, you could sneak in something a bit experimental, like no-rules football, or a wide-awake-athon (staying up all night — this should only be attempted during a long holiday). Are your activities often directly spiritual, i.e. Bible quizzes? Well, try doing something which isn't so spiritually-minded, like swimming or ping-pong volleyball. All of these ideas can easily be adapted for smaller groups.

The name of the game is experimentation, and being enormously enthusiastic. If your style and demeanour suggest that some new activity will be a flop and a total drag, then it will be an uphill struggle to get anyone to join in. But if you behave as though it's brilliant, amazing, hilarious and about to take the world by storm, then you will at least get some young people sufficiently intrigued to take part. Then if it's a flop and a total drag, it was their fault for not really trying ...

Each week, have an active sport, an arty or cerebral event and a coffee bar, as well as the traditional table tennis and snooker. Obviously, if you have a small group, you don't need to provide all the activities on one evening, but when you have about 25 or so young people, you need to be reckoning that three activities at once is a minimum.

# Variety in the Programme

Here is a suggested programme for one school term, which is far from perfect, but which has been put together following the principles of variety, having something for everyone, exercising body, mind, and spirit, and having a good laugh in the process. Most weeks table tennis, snooker, table football, badminton, the coffee bar and a video are provided as standard, then in addition:

| Date | Activity | Workshop | Mellow Moments |
|------|----------|----------|----------------|
| Sept 14 | Football Championship | Catering | Volleyball |
| Sept 21 | Table Tennis Tournament | Pebble Painting | Chill Out |
| Sept 28 | Super Shuttle (badminton) | Aerobics | Worship and Communion |
| Oct 5 | Sussex Young Teens Celebration : Bus leaves at 1.30 p.m. | | |
| Oct 12 | Tin Can Alley | Catering | Football |
| Oct 19 | Not the Pancake Day | Trivial Pursuit | *Discussion:* Okay 2 B Gay? |
| Oct 26 | Great Duna-Movie Experience: Popcorn, ice creams, etc. and a good video | | |
| Nov 2 | Scalextric Speed Trials | Top of the Pops | *Seminar:* Homelessness |
| Nov 9 | Indoor Cricket | Catering | Chill Out |
| Nov 16 | Snooker Championship | Crafty Cards | *Seminar:* Your gift of healing |
| Nov 23 | Football Penalty Competition | Make Decorations | Worship and Communion |
| Nov 30 | The Pool Shoot-out | Creative Dance | Football |
| Dec 7 | Sussex Young Teens Celebration: Bus leaves at 5.30 p.m. | | |
| Dec 14 | Netball | Men's Catering | *YP Seminars* |
| Dec 21 | Ice Rink & Lights Outing (return by 9 p.m.) | | Gift Exchange |

The programme has to contain combinations of all these

elements in order to maintain its sparkle and flair. The development of a successful programme takes a lot of careful planning. It's no good trying to have a wide game in the local park if it will be dark by the time you get there (unless it's a wide game in the dark), or if the park will be thronging with football supporters.

As you can see, the plan is to have a Catering Workshop regularly, because they are popular, but to vary the programme with sports, games, new activities, old favourites and then break it up even more with off-site events, such as the trip to the Ice Rink and the twice-a-term Young Teens Celebrations, which are excellent opportunities for young people from a number of churches in the county to gather in large numbers for fun and games, worship and teaching. The bus ride is part of the fun.

I recognise that some youth groups are not sufficiently large to run as many activities as that. But surely, finding a variety of things to do when you cannot offer so many each week makes the job easier, not more difficult. Lack of space can create problems, but there is usually a way round, especially in the summer months, when the wide outdoors beckons.

# Chapter Nine
# **Communication Skills**

Communication depends on both the deliverer and the receiver of the message using the same medium according to the same rules. The person with a message cannot convey the message to the receiver without using the right means of communication. Semaphore is of little use on radio; if your audience only understands Flemish, then even the simplest instructions given in any other language will be a waste of breath.

When speaking to groups of people — especially groups of teenagers — you need to be aware of the fact that different members of the audience are at different stages in their learning process. Some are doing well at school; perhaps a few are bright but disinterested; others are more suited for work as roof beams or mine supports. Being aware of the mix in your youth group is the first stage in attempting to communicate with them meaningfully.

In addition to an appreciation of their learning and concentration abilities, you need also to establish a relationship with the young people, so that you have friendship and acceptance working with you in your attempts to teach and train them. It is of vital importance that you get to know the young people in your care before you begin to speak into their lives. It is my view that some school teachers can find themselves bearing little fruit, partly because, say, history, is by its very nature tedious and irrelevant. They are totally sunk, because it is impossible to convince a mob of twelve-year-olds that the Black Prince, the Treaty of Versailles or Perkin Warbeck are even remotely interesting.

Our job is easier, because Jesus Christ is powerfully relevant to daily life, and therefore we should be able to communicate more effectively. But we need also to get over the difficulty of the young people's expectation of our teaching times to be similar to history lessons. If we impart dry information to our group in a classroom style, we will generally fail to plant seeds of truth in many hearts. But if we have established friendships with the young people, we will be able to speak much more effectively into their lives, 'scratching where they itch', and being powerfully relevant.

If members of your group are experiencing persecution at school, then some appropriate comments will be very helpful; a thesis on the life of Jonah, who rebelled against God and ran away from his calling, would be mildly interesting, but not strongly profitable at that particular time. See what I mean? Even if you disagree with me decrying any fascination with the story of Marie Celeste burning the cakes at the battle of the Little Big Horn, or whatever she did, you have to admit that taking up themes which apply directly to the current experience of your group is a fine idea.

Moving gently on, we come to the issue of preaching. Or rather, we don't. Preaching is what adults listen to on Sundays in church. Preaching is what young people don't listen to on Sundays in church.

To communicate with a young people's group, it is important to avoid formality, or anything that even hints of a school atmosphere, since that carries with it all the negative connotations which are unlikely to help young people receive the Word with joy, or apply it to their lives. It would be in danger of becoming another *being talked at* session, like a physics theory double lesson or, worse yet, an assembly.

# Preparing a message

You may well be giving your talk as part of a series (working through a biblical book, or covering a theme in some depth). If this is the case, the title and main theme of the talk will already be established. If this is a one-off talk, or something to fill in between series, then the same principles apply. Please avoid deciding what you want to talk about, but decide what you feel the young people need to be hearing about, with suitable reference to the rest of your team.

- Pray for God to inspire you as you come to your preparation. He is eager to communicate truth to the young people. Give it plenty of time. I find that two hours' preparation is about right for a 20-minute talk, as long as the two hours are several days in advance of the talk. This gives you the opportunity to polish, or re-write(!) Sometimes, when the topic is not one with which you are familiar, or the passage is difficult (I once tackled a special series on *The Hard Sayings of Jesus*), more time will be needed for background research and reading.

- Read the passage, or find a passage that centres on the topic. I am constantly turning to my trusty concordance (a heavy-weight tome which lists all the words used in the Bible, and gives references for where they can be found), and to *Vine's Expository Dictionary* (a brilliant book which gives the meanings of the Greek words used, the way in which they were used, and other references, where the words were used in a similar way). This is because my brain is contained within a skull which takes a six and seven-eighths hat, and therefore cannot adequately store all the information I need. The trick is in knowing where to find out the things you don't know.

- Read the passage again. Then read it in another version. Be aware of the various versions of the Bible your young people use, and centre on the one used by the majority. This may mean constant reference to other scholarly works. Look up words you don't know in a dictionary, or, better still, in a dictionary of Bible words. Focus on the parts of the passage or theme that excite you. If you are not excited, you won't sustain the preparation, and by the time you come to deliver your message, you will be bored, and so will the young people who are listening to you.

- Structure your talk in the most logical way, concentrating on the main section. What is your main point? If the young people go away thinking about one thing, what would you like that one thing to be? Don't worry about having three points; the youngsters will probably remember only one; so just have one. This will help keep the length of your talk down, as well. Don't worry, at this stage, about how to begin your talk, or about any appeal or challenge you want to bring at the end. A good rule of thumb is that if the main point is thoroughly researched, prepared, and is well delivered, the intro and 'outro' will be easy to sort out later.

- Make sure your talk is correct theologically. Look up the passage in a Bible commentary, and see what scholars have thought about the issues. You may want to chat it through with your homegroup leader, or a church leader. But remember, they may not be gifted with the young teens age group, so tread carefully if they give you pointers for your delivery.
- Do your best to think of a good illustration of the main point — this will bring your talk to life. If it's something to which the young people can relate, so much the better. Remember the age of the group — don't rely on them knowing all about something which is ancient history to them, like the invention of pocket calculators, the Amoco Cadiz disaster, or the influence of the New Romantics in bringing about the premature demise of the punk era. (What?)
- Plan how you will introduce your topic. Find a good way to relax yourself into the talk, and to help the young people overlook any nervousness you may be feeling. A joke or something would be ideal. Don't worry if it's not too relevant, so much the better if it is. Worry a lot if it's not too funny, since no one will laugh, unless they laugh at you.
- Practice. I used to stand in front of a full-length mirror and deliver my talk, with one eye on my notes, one eye on the clock, and one eye on the mirror. This, eventually, made my head ache. So in the end I just preached in front of the mirror, with one eye on my notes, and the other eye on the mirror (but sneakily glancing at the clock from time to time). Seriously, this practice makes you feel very silly at first, but helps to identify a number of things.

Firstly, you may discover that your main point isn't all that convincing, or that you don't quite see how your illustration fits the theme. It's a shame to discover glaring flaws in front of your audience. At least you will have time to put things right before the appointed hour ...

Secondly, timing. I would have thought that 20 minutes would be a good sort of time at which you should be aiming, if you are a beginner. More experienced speakers can manage 30 minutes, but if your talk takes much longer than that, the young people won't be able to concentrate very well. Only top-flight, seriously gifted speakers can keep an audience of teenagers gripped for longer than this. So, how long did you take? Some people will have flannelled on and on, while others will have petered out within a very few minutes of starting.

If your talk is too long, be ruthless and cut it without mercy. While it is good to read widely and to prepare more than you will need, it is important to know that the background material needs to be just that — background — and not become points 7 to 43 of your lecture. If you need to expand your talk, add a couple more Scripture references (young people take a while to look up verses), or try speaking with more deliberation, pausing more often, and waiting for the laughter and applause to die down (you should be so lucky!).

Thirdly, you may realise that you wave your arms about like a windmill when all you meant to do was to make a gesture. Or perhaps it was difficult for you to keep looking up at the mirror because you were tied mercilessly to your notes. In either case, practise making helpful, illustrative hand movements which give more impact to your point. Gestures should obey two simple rules; they should be larger than life, so that the people in the back row can see them; and they should be controlled, so that you don't blast the poor fellow in the front row into the middle of next week.

And now a true story. I was sitting at home, reading through my notes before going to an important meeting at which I was the speaker. I thought to myself, 'The last thing I want to do is to leave my notes behind.' So, sure enough, the last thing I did as I shut the front door and went off to the meeting, was to leave my notes behind! Fortunately, I had a draft copy tucked into my Bible, and I had enough presence of mind to adjust as I spoke. But it was a harsh way to learn a simple lesson.

The day arrives, and you are ready to give your talk. Pray that God would speak through you, and that the most memorable part of the talk will be the main point, not the illustration, the jokes, the nervous tic you developed after eleven seconds, or the strange choking sound you made as you fell over backwards, having forgotten to breathe. No one's as bad as all that ...

# Delivering your talk

The key to good delivery is confidence, and you will have gained tremendous amounts of this as you challenged your mirror to confess its sin, to believe in the story of Jonah, or whatever it is you are speaking about. Two aphorisms spring to mind: practice makes perfect, and competence gives confidence. In other words, if you have spoken well to the mirror, you ought to be able to do a good job in front of the young people. There will be distractions to which you are not used — a simple cough can throw you completely, while the trumpet blast of a nose clearance job can finish you altogether, but try to press on. Be real, since no one expects you to be Billy Graham or Dr Martyn Lloyd-Jones or, least of all, Ben Elton. If God has called you to the task, He will anoint you with the gift of being able to communicate. If God hasn't called you, you will know four minutes after you start your talk!

Since you have already gone to all the trouble of setting up an overhead projector for the worship time, use the OHP to illustrate your talk with either the talk outline, or some jolly pictures. You could even write out the key verse(s), and project them for all to see, which helps keep the concentration of the young people.

Listen to the Holy Spirit as you speak, and ask Him to give you words of knowledge, so that when you come to the application of the talk, there will be some punch for members of your group. What is the point if it doesn't touch anyone? It's just an exercise in mental agility (which is not a waste of time, but a lot less than you had expected).

I once read a very worthy magazine article which was an exposition of 1 Corinthians 14, describing the way Paul wanted the church to exercise spiritual gifts, ministering to one another, and yet keeping things in good order. It was a brilliant article, and truly inspiring until the final sentence. The author stated that while this passage was a good description of how the church in the New Testament had worshipped and lived, the apostolic dispensation had ceased with the death of Paul, and so it was only of academic interest to us as Christians in the twentieth century. Disaster!

This sort of approach to Bible study is not only spiritually bankrupt, it also communicates to young people that the Bible is strictly irrelevant for them today, and that it is just another intellectual exercise, like learning Latin, or remembering those cunning maths formulas.

I can safely declare that I have never once in all my adult years used the method for solving quadratic equations I religiously memorised for my O level. My life just isn't the sort of life where x squared comes up a lot, and I never have to divide by the cosine of 45 radians, whatever they are, to be quite honest with you. I suppose I always knew it wouldn't be the sort of information I would need for health and happiness, so that's why maths seemed academic and lifeless for me. What a tragedy it would be if we allowed our young people to have the same dowdy, low opinion of the Holy Scriptures, the revelation of God!

# Leading a Bible study group

One of the advantages of being a small youth group is that you can have a good knowledge of each individual, and that you can let small-group dynamics work for you. Encouraging the young people to read the Bible for themselves, and to discover the truth through a well-directed discussion time, is very valuable indeed.

The basic difference between speaking to a group and leading a group in discussion is, of course, the amount of speaking done by the leader. If you like, you can preach a sermon to the small group, and they will learn, depending on your content, ability to communicate, style, and their receptivity and willingness to concentrate.

But if you choose to lead a discussion, the young people will be teaching each other from the Bible, and it is a well-known fact that young people are far more interested in each other's opinions and comments than in those of their youth leaders.

So, how can you get the discussion going, and how can you keep it from developing in the wrong directions?

Firstly, decide what passage of Scripture you intend to study together, and read it through carefully. Then, divide the passage up into logical sections, giving each section a heading. Then turn each heading into a question (panic not, I have provided an example for you to follow). These are your provocative discussion-starters, so they must be questions which demand thought and a good answer, not 'yes' or 'no' questions. Monosyllabic response is unacceptable.

It is the last thing you want. Right? Yes. Good. See what I mean? The fact is, that the more you get the group to say, the less you will have to say, and the more they will learn from the Word. Ask 'how?' or 'why?' which helps them read the text, see the facts and grasp the point of it. As they work hard, read the verse and think of what to say, their minds will be filled with the truth.

Impressive or what? All of that bit was in monosyllables. But I'll stop now. My point is that social skills will be given an opportunity to develop if we help the young people to thrash through some doctrinal issues and discover what the Bible teaches.

If your discussion-starters don't work, then you need to provoke answers with guiding questions to encourage thoughts along the right lines. The value of this style of questioning is that you can maintain control over the direction of the conversation, bringing it back to the subject whenever it drifts.

Here is my example of how to prepare for the discussion. Let's say the passage we are studying is Ephesians 2:1–10. Firstly, I divide the passage into sections:

vv. 1–3   How we used to live.
vv. 4–7   What God has done for us.
vv. 8–9   How God did this.
v. 10     Why God did this.

These become questions very simply:

vv. 1–3   How did we used to live?
vv. 4–7   What has God done for us?
vv. 8–9   How did God do this?
v. 10     Why did God do this?

And guiding questions help the discussion along, and bring clarity where the text is difficult or needs explanation:

vv. 1–3  What are the ways of this world? Who is the 'ruler of the air'? Why is he given this title? What does 'gratifying' mean? How did we do this? How does the Devil work in us? How can we prevent him from doing so? Does anyone have any testimonies to share about this?

vv. 4–7  Why did God make us alive? What does 'dead in transgressions' mean? In what ways are we seated with Christ in the heavenly realms? What are the implications for our behaviour if we are seated with Him? What qualities of God's character are mentioned in this passage? How can we apply His character to our lives? In what ways are we like Him already?

vv. 8–9  What saved us, the blood of Christ, or grace? Are works of any value at all?

v. 10  What are the 'attributes' of workmanship? What is the purpose of our existence? Do we have free will, or are we programmed to do good works? What are some of the good works God has prepared for us?

While this is far less than perfect, it is a helpful way to promote Godly discussion on the subject of the Scripture passage. Clearly, this method also requires a degree of preparation; it would be wise to have a general idea of the kinds of answers you are anticipating.

Many Scripture passages lend themselves to this sort of treatment (divide the passage into sections, give the sections headings, and turn the headings into questions). Here are a few passages which will be of help to you as you practise this technique, and will be of help to your young people as they discover the truth for themselves.

It seems that the theological ones are best for this, partly because many of the stories are self-explanatory, and partly because the passages which are theological lend themselves to thorough examination, since they are so packed with content. Having said that, the first of these passages contains Jesus' parables of the lost sheep, coin and son — parables can be helpfully unravelled.

Luke 15:1–32.
> Lost by nature; lost by circumstance; lost by choice.

1 Cor. 11:17–34.
> How communion meetings were run; the symbolic meal; the exam; the conclusions.

Phil. 1:3–11.
> Paul's thanksgiving; Paul's personal comments; Paul's prayer.

2 Tim. 3:1–17.
> The marks of disobedience; Paul's testimony; how to be wise.

On other occasions, it may be more suitable to take a theme, rather than basing your studies in one passage of Scripture. There are a variety of themes which can be explored, such as salvation, God's love, the shedding of blood, holiness. Have two or three Scriptures ready, to fuel your discussions, to give content to your opinions, or to counter ungodly attitudes or responses.

You may wish to consider

*Wisdom:* James 3:17; Prov. 2:1–5; 1 Kings 3:16–28.
> This can lead into discussion about making good decisions when faced with moral or ethical choices.

*Sacrifice:* Heb. 9:16–22; Lev. 17:11; Col. 1:15–20.
> Discuss God's high opinion of salvation, His attitude to sin and His ability to save us.

*Healing:* Acts 3:1–10; Mark 7:31–37; John 11:32–44.
> Discuss the reality of healing; ask for testimonies; pray for the sick.

*The Body of Christ:* 1 Cor. 12:12–26; Eph. 4:11–16; Phil. 2:1–4.
> Help the young people understand that if they are Christians, then they belong to the body of Christ — there are implications, privileges and responsibilities.

Beware of some of the dangers into which discussion-group leaders can fall. Don't get into a scene where you ask a question of one of the young people, and they answer you. Then you ask another person another question. They reply, and so it goes on, like a boring, non-interactive quiz, where everyone gets brassed off rather quickly. Secondly, avoid getting into conversation with one or two of the vocal members of the group, so much so that the others start chatting among themselves to stave off the boredom of your elevated debate. Thirdly, avoid allowing the group to be dominated by the talkative ones. Bring in the quiet people by asking them direct questions if you need to do so, or asking their opinion on what someone else has just said.

Handling wrong answers without just saying 'no' is easy. Use phrases like, 'What do you others think?' or, 'Is that what the passage says?' Try to let the others point out errors, unless they do so in a put-down way, which will effectively close the mouth of any young person who is even slightly shy.

# Discussion topics

There are many ethical issues which can give rise to helpful application, such as animal rights, vandalism, homelessness, alcoholism, abortion, homosexuality, the bomb, racism, vegetarianism, voluntary euthanasia, feminism, drug abuse, AIDS, etc. While it may appear that there are few biblical references which can be brought to bear on some of these topics, it may be helpful for your group to discover how to discuss, to give voice to their feelings and opinions on something where they are comfortable with the topic, and then for you to go on to discussing something more theological, once they have got the hang of the techniques and style of conversation required.

My experience is that young people are packed with views and opinions, some of which are legitimate, and some of which are rooted in error and bias, in my opinion. But I find it very worrying to hear thirteen-year-olds confidently telling me that humans need to eat meat to survive, or that there are many circumstances where it's okay to have an abortion, or that they know people who were born with homosexual genes. I don't object to them having an opinion which differs from mine, but I cannot allow them to continue in ignorance and prejudice.

Discussions give young people a chance to be heard, a chance to be respected and a chance to be agreed with. Many young people are used to an anarchistic style of discussion where they are shouted down, put down, or laughed at. So create a setting where adult behaviour is encouraged. For instance, when discussing the topic 'OK 2 B Gay?' the first half-minute was set aside for sniggering and smirking; thereafter, it was banned, and we were able to discuss the issues without silliness or mockery. It may have been difficult to talk about the seriousness of sexual sin in the context of giggles or people referring to 'poofs' and 'nancy-boys'. Good conclusions were reached, and we decided that we should be compassionate to people as people, whatever sins they committed.

# Leading evangelistic discussion groups

Once again, the dynamic of a small group can be used to good effect, as you invite the young people to share their feelings and thoughts about the existence of God, the value of the Bible, the reality of the life of Jesus, the meaning of the cross and the challenge to radical discipleship.

I have found that many of the non-Christian young people who come through our doors are woefully ignorant of any facts about God, Jesus Christ, the Bible or church practice. Many are astonished at our worship times, and often are full of questions and comments — 'Why do you clap and dance?' 'Why do you believe the Bible?' 'I've never been anywhere like this before!' 'Something was happening ...!' Others quietly listen to the comments, prayers and songs, considering these amazing truths for the first time. It is interesting to speak to them as they try to grasp the weight of what they are encountering.

An educating process is needed in order for these people to understand that they are sinful, need to repent and accept the salvation that is offered to them. This process is often difficult for us, since many of our contacts lack grey matter, but it is necessary.

It is clearly a much more free-ranging discussion, but it still needs to be directed (and re-directed when it goes off the point), and everyone should be brought in to express their opinion. It can be helpful to have other Christians in the group, so that they can chip in with a burst of truth, to deny the opinions and misconceptions that are being thrown into the maelstrom of the discussion. A testimony can be very powerful in this setting, giving the young people an opportunity to ask questions and find out what they want to know, as well as what we believe they need to know.

Perhaps you could start an evangelistic discussion with some provocative questions. 'Do you believe in God, or not, and why?' 'Are rules necessary?' 'Do you believe in heaven?' 'Do you believe in hell?' 'Who was Jesus?' 'Have you ever read any of the Bible for your own interest?' 'Do your parents have any religious views?' 'Why do you think we worship God in the way we do?' 'Suppose I thought it was okay to steal things, and I stole your bike or ghetto blaster. I think it's okay. Any problems?'

# Leading worship with young people

There are many different opinions on the subject of worship; there are probably as many different opinions as there are worshippers! But be that as it may, I shall venture my own view and leave it to you to abandon, adapt or adopt the style which I have found to be very useful. I do not suggest that this is the precise way you should lead worship; I only offer the lessons I have learned along the way.

It's easier to lead adults in worship than young people! In many churches, the adults are ready and willing to worship, and they approach the throne of grace with enthusiasm and abandon. That's also true of young people, but only after they have been taught to do so, and given plenty of opportunity to practise!

We must be willing to worship God as He desires.

*Yet a time is coming and has now come when the true worshippers will worship the Father in spirit and truth, for they are the kind of worshippers the Father seeks* (John 4:23).

How's this for a contrast? I grew up attending a young people's fellowship which had a regular sing-song — *Kum By*

*Yah* sung loudly was the nearest we ever got to revival fire falling. I learned that the best way to get things going was to sing the faster songs first, and then attempt the slower, draggy ones. Yes, folks, this was the level at which we were operating; no one ever called it worship, so we didn't have much expectation; besides, the only model we had to follow was the *hymn, prayer, stand up, sit down, one finger, one thumb, keep moving, one arm, one leg, one nod of the head* of Evensong.

Young people need to have a definite focus or purpose to what they do; they will become bored very quickly if they are unaware of your intention to lead them into the presence of God.

Without a stated goal, it will be just a sing-song, except some of the words will have a religious feel to them. It is now my belief that we should follow the pattern of worship laid down in the Psalms and through the various other biblical references to worship. This is far beyond the scope of this book, and far wiser minds than mine have been exercised over the most appropriate and suitable forms of worship.

Begin by praising God for who He is and for what He has done, generally. The Bible contains many passages which call us to give praise and honour to the King of Kings.

> *I will be glad and rejoice in you; I will sing praise to your name, O Most High* (Ps. 9:2).
> *... my tongue will sing of your righteousness* (Ps. 51:14).
> *Praise our God, O peoples, let the sound of his praise be heard* (Ps. 66:8).

It may be seen that this is Objective Praise, a grateful, rejoicing statement of God's goodness, holiness, love or faithfulness. It need not be directly related to individuals. It is like a call to God's presence. Suitable songs include: *Come, let us sing; There is power in the name of Jesus; God is good; Hosanna; Glory, glory in the highest.*

This leads us towards expressing our thanksgiving to God for His relevance to us personally. I was reading somewhere about the names of God. *Yahweh* emphasises the gulf between the Holy God of Heaven and sinful men, while *Adonai* emphasises God's love and acceptance of us as His children. The Bible uses

*Adonai* five times for every time it uses *Yahweh*. God is holy and awesome, but He loves us with an everlasting love, and He accepts us warts and all.

The Bible encourages us to enter boldly into the outer courts of God's presence with singing, shouting and dancing, and to thank Him for His personal impact on our lives. For example:

> *I will sing to the Lord, for he has been good to me* (Ps. 13:6).
> *The Lord gives strength to his people; the Lord blesses his people with peace* (Ps. 29:11).
> *He fulfils the desires of those who fear him; he hears their cry and saves them* (Ps. 145:19).

Suitable songs for this part of the praise time are: *Oooooh heaven is in my heart; Shout for joy and sing; Jehovah Jireh; Father God I wonder; Great is the Lord and most worthy of praise.*

Once we have focused our attention on God, we can begin to tell Him how much we love Him, to adore and bow down before Him in heartfelt worship.

God loves to hear our voices as we sing, but He looks on the heart, and is not going to be fooled by body posture. Nevertheless, young people need to be reminded about raising their hands to Him as a demonstration of their need of Him. Some may want to kneel; others will perhaps express emotion as they worship. This follows the biblical pattern of singing, seeking the face of God, and taking refuge in Him.

> *Speak to one another with psalms, hymns and spiritual songs. Sing and make music in your heart to the Lord, always giving thanks to God the Father for everything, in the name of our Lord Jesus Christ* (Eph. 5:19).
> *I have sought your face with all my heart; be gracious to me according to your promise* (Ps. 119:58).
> *In you, O Lord, I have taken refuge; let me never be put to shame* (Ps. 71:1).

These Scriptures speak of total commitment to a God who is totally committed to us. They speak of love and worship and honour. It is our pleasant task to be worshippers of the Living

God. Suitable songs for heartfelt worship are numerous: *Lord, you are so precious to me; All heaven declares; Glorious Father, we exalt you; More love, more power; When I look into your holiness; My Lord, what love is this?* etc.

Many times of worship will continue into a ministry time, as God inspires us with prophecies, words of knowledge, insight, a teaching, or other spiritual gifts. For more comments and testimony of our experience of spiritual gifts, please turn to the chapter on *Charismatic Life*. But not yet.

At other times, it can be very helpful to move from heartfelt expressions of adoration into a time of declaring our purpose to serve God with our lives, and to be an army, taking territory from the enemy. Prophetic songs include: *Rejoice, rejoice!; Rise up, you champions of God; Worldchangers; Shine, Jesus, shine; Be bold, be strong.*

But the object of a time of praise and worship is not to follow the pattern religiously (we ought not to do anything religiously, except perhaps avoid formality and ceremonial), but to enter the Holy of Holies and to give God the honour. Only God can judge a worship time — 'good' or otherwise — since if He is exalted, then He is pleased.

I make a point (as far as is possible) of explaining what is happening as it happens — some young people may be unused to our charismatic style, and therefore an explanation, albeit brief, about speaking in tongues or about prophecy can clarify something which might otherwise cause confusion. It can also help to give reasons why we shout and dance for joy, since those with a religious background may be shocked or surprised (or both) by our exuberance and freedom.

It can sometimes help to put the chairs away. This has two major benefits: it creates the space needed for dancing, moving about, intermingling and can sometimes encourage a friendlier, less formal atmosphere; and it prevents all but the most determined from sitting down! It can be very frustrating for a worship leader to find that as soon as the first song is over, most of the young people have stopped participating and are sitting down. It is more likely that the young people will remain involved in the worship if they are standing. When there isn't time to put the chairs away, or we choose not to do so, I consistently invite the young people to stand as they sing and worship.

Encourage the worshippers to raise their hands to God, which expresses our devotion to Him and our desire of Him. And everyone will be able to concentrate more with their eyes shut if the songs are well known. Worship leaders need to learn how to worship with their eyes open, so that they can see what God is doing among the young people, and can discourage any who are chatting.

When singing in tongues (singing in the Spirit), it is helpful to explain what is happening with a few words like, 'If God's gifted you with a language you have never learned, or a praise language you can use to worship Him, then this would be a good time to exercise your gift. If you haven't got that gift, then not to worry, just continue in worship.'

Some young people are very eager to bring a contribution to the meeting as they hear from God. Others need to be encouraged strongly. Both of these groups can be served by inviting contributions several times.

Make a comment like, 'If God has been speaking to you, and you think He wants us all to receive the benefit of what He is saying, then now would be a good time to come to the front, share it with one of the team and then use the microphone to tell everyone.' This can have the same effect as the little boy who pulled his finger out of the hole in the dam.

I make a point of thanking those who contribute. This is simple courtesy.

A word about music. The original meaning of the word *psalm* is 'a striking or twitching of the fingers (on musical strings)'. It is clear that a vital element of a psalm, then, is the music, and not just the words.

Music speaks to the spirit and the emotions, as words speak to the mind and the will. There's a generalisation for you. But it is clear that songs in a minor key can often be sadder than those in a major key (let's get technical for a moment).

There is no such thing as a Hebrew- or Russian-sounding tune that isn't in a minor key, and everything by Ian White is in major sevenths. But I think you'll agree that all Country and Western music should be outlawed, since it is loathsome.

I have discovered, much to my amazement, that the young people can happily worship without any instruments. They manage well with just an acoustic guitar, and they love it when the full band pumps up the volume. It is really very simple: if they want to worship, then they will. If they don't, then it may be hard work persuading them to worship against their will! But I do my best to provide a solid musical backing to worship, simply because I want to give the young people every encouragement to honour the Lord.

Musicians need to have a certain level of skill, or their mistakes (wrong notes, getting out of time, knocking over the drum kit, for example) may be distracting. Youngsters are used, after all, to hearing music, played by serious professionals, which has been made to sound perfect in recording studios at the cost of grillions of megadollars. This does not mean that we need to emulate this in every way(!), but it does suggest that every effort we can make to be lively, modern and reasonably competent would be warmly appreciated. It may also be important to note that the current music scene relies heavily on up-to-date instruments, so the local psychedelic experience band comprising Mellotron, Hawaiian and Flamenco guitars, tuba and kettle drum may prove to be inadequate.

Having said all that, I feel that one of the main reasons why we worship God is that we want to honour Him corporately. This means that I am motivated to encourage the young people to praise and worship God, not just to sing the songs. There may be some in the group who want to stay on the sidelines; there may be some who are easily distracted and need to have another opportunity to put their attention on the Lord; there may be some who are true worshippers, and who will be right there, eyes shut, hands and voices raised, giving God His due and receiving blessing from the throne of grace. It really does take all sorts, and you need to decide the point at which you leave the sideliners out and keep going forward with the worshippers.

Worship is not just the singing of songs, even though I may have appeared to suggest this. Consider the following ideas: try reading the words aloud from the overhead (use an overhead, since this keeps the hands free for clapping, dancing and raising); have a few moments of silence before the Lord; lead the young people in prayer; encourage one or two of the young people to lead out in prayer or read passages from the Bible; pray aloud together all at once on a theme; applaud God; invite short prayers of thanksgiving, one after another. Be a little bit experimental and find out what works with your group. Youngsters are always being told to be quiet — at school, at home, even in your meetings — so why not shout your praise to the Lord? Give them some content, such as 'The Lord is good! His love endures forever!' and tell them to shout and bellow. It's fun, it's reverent, it's free!

Whatever happens, the focus of the time should be the Lord Jesus, the God of creation, the Holy Spirit, and the work the Trinity has done in each of our lives. Give Him room to move, and be expectant.

I realise that all this may be boringly obvious to many youth-group leaders, and that it may be frighteningly radical and impossible for others. I assure you that it is not only possible, it is God's desire for our worship.

> *What then shall we say, brothers? When you come together, everyone has a hymn, or a word of instruction, a revelation, a tongue or an interpretation. All of these must be done for the strengthening of the church* (1 Cor. 14:26).
> *God has ascended amid shouts of joy, the Lord among the sounding of the trumpets. Sing praises to God, sing praises; sing praises to our King, sing praises. For God is the King of all the earth; sing to him a psalm of praise* (Ps. 47:5–7).

Let's be ready and willing to joyfully worship the Lord our God. Let's be prepared to teach our young people to do the same.

# Chapter Ten
# **Charismatic Life**

We should expect the Holy Spirit to be meeting us in our worship times. This is not the aim of our worship — we give God honour because He deserves all our praise and adoration — but it is a supernatural side-effect; God responds to us, and warfare is done in the heavenly places. Let's encourage young people to participate in the meetings. While they need to be well led, they should not be dominated by leaders or musicians.

The gifts of the Holy Spirit can be categorised thus:

- the power to *know* — gifts of wisdom, knowledge and distinguishing spirits;
- the power to *say* — gifts of prophecy, tongues and interpretation;
- the power to *do* — gifts of faith, healing and miraculous powers.

There are also the 'ministry gifts':

> It was he who gave some to be apostles, some to be prophets, some to be evangelists, and some to be pastors and teachers ... (Eph. 4:11).

I believe that these ministry gifts are still being given by God to His people, as He equips the church for the work of service (not the work of services, mind!) There is a distinction between someone who prophesies and a prophet; surely the latter is more significantly and consistently gifted.

Other passages of Scripture point to further gifts, such as hospitality, martyrdom, serving, encouraging, leading, mercy, celibacy; obviously, we do not dismiss these, but I want to focus attention on gifts which are more usually seen in the context of worship meetings.

The gifts of the Spirit are not to be limited to use in meetings, but we should nevertheless be aware of the vital part the exercising of these gifts can play as we worship the Lord and receive teaching from the Word.

I have an expectation that God will to speak to His people through prophecy or words of knowledge or wisdom as we meet to pray and worship. This is high-risk stuff! The memories are brilliant, and the long-term impact is wonderful. I believe that into order to encourage the young people to use spiritual gifts, we should give the lead ourselves, prophesying over them and being bold in our prayer for healing and deliverance. I find it very exciting to be in a meeting where church leaders are exercising spiritual gifts; it edifies me, and it encourages me to do the same. When the young people observe their leaders exercising spiritual gifts, then they are also encouraged.

My own testimony is that I spoke with boldness at a meeting, prophesying the word of the Lord over the young people. Just a few weeks later, two young men were stirring up the gift of prophecy within them and being similarly bold. There is clearly a need for controls when you are dealing with gifts which, after all, the enemy can counterfeit. I encourage the teenagers to share their contributions with leaders before they declare them publicly, to give us an opportunity to correct or balance their words, or ask them to wait for a more appropriate time in the meeting.

I have been in many meetings where young people have fallen over in a swoon as the Holy Spirit touches them. It is as if there is a Holy anaesthetic being administered, and they collapse in a heap. A youthful tendency to compete in this area can be very unhelpful; and there has, on occasion, been a need to rebuke the young people for spectating. There is a need to be 'in control' when you have a meeting; and the Scripture warns us that everything should be done decently and in good order. But to be too quick to censure could be a mistake. The learning process is a gradual one, as I found a balance between observing and controlling. It was best to proceed slowly, blessing what God was doing, asking God for gifts of discernment and being alert for the counterfeit.

One of the most memorable occasions was when perhaps 40% of the people present were lying on the floor, enjoying

God's calm presence. Some were being prayed for, while others were left to their own devices. I felt strongly that there should not be any imbalance, and I was keen to maintain equal emphasis on the Spirit and the Word. So I stood up to preach, and managed to hold the attention of those who were still on the planet. About halfway through my talk, one of the lads began to slump sideways in his chair. With a gentle sigh, he fell to the floor. 'Thanks, Tony!' I said, totally thrown off my point. Later, Tony jokingly told me that as he began to swoon in the Spirit, God had spoken to him, saying, 'Go on, it's all right. It's only Andy Back, and he's rubbish!' Tony was only kidding. Actually, it was quite a good talk.

Experiences vary widely as God deals supernaturally with young people: some become acutely burdened for the lost; others are released into great joy and celebration. Others simply have a good time alone with Him as He speaks into their lives. Others are released into gifts of prophecy or tongues. Young people who have before been slightly unreliable have become strong, mature and fervent in their walk with the Lord. They are not sinless, but they are much more consistent. God spoke to one girl about her relationship with her older brother. At the same time, her brother was getting the same treatment! When they spoke about it afterwards, they realised that God was very serious about their arguments, teasing and general sibling antagonism. Their relationship changed from that very night, and, three years later, seems to have gone from strength to strength. They now share excellent fellowship as well as family love.

## Results are more important

I am looking for long-term effect, and not just physical manifestations. I thank God for shaking, trembling, knee-vibrations, hip-shimmies, swooning and all the other strange and wonderful physical effects that the Holy Spirit's power can have on a person. But I thank God far more for the dynamic impact God has on lives, changing convictions, healing old wounds, turning attitudes around, causing repentance, giving youngsters a heart for evangelism or worship or a gift of intercession or whatever.

With a realistic view of the physical aspects, I have developed this policy through trial and error, really, and have found that protracted times of prayer, with lots of other well-meaning young people gathering round, can be very unhelpful. This can turn things into a bit of a circus, with all the associated difficulties of mixed-gender prayer times, which are to be avoided. This happens particularly when prayer for healing follows a specific word of knowledge, and faith and expectancy are high.

Stand to one side, and ask God to give discernment or knowledge of what is happening; if God hasn't finished, then either join in the prayer ministry, if that is appropriate, or leave things be for a few minutes, and then come back. If you feel the Lord's work is done, then boldly step in, and ask what God has been doing. You may want to lead in a concluding prayer of thanksgiving, or with a prayer asking God to continue His work over the next few days.

Other demonstrations of the activity of the Holy Spirit include faith, healing, prophecy and words of knowledge. I have seen many occasions when teaching has been accompanied by spiritual activity, with words of wisdom and knowledge being shared as part of the prepared message, which leads me to restate an important point: prayerful preparation is vital, and can be used by the Lord to great effect.

Please exercise a bold caution; alternatively, please be warily forthright.

> *Do not put out the Spirit's fire; do not treat prophecies with contempt. Test everything. Hold on to the good. Avoid every kind of evil. May God himself, the God of peace, sanctify you through and through. May your whole spirit, soul and body be kept blameless at the coming of our Lord Jesus Christ. The one who calls you is faithful and he will do it* (1 Thess. 5:19–24).

Paul promises that we will be helped by God as we do our best to walk in wisdom and blamelessness, without mistreating prophecies or, as some of the other translations put it, quenching the Holy Spirit.

## Chapter Eleven
# Evangelism or Pastoring?

One of the most important decisions you will ever face as a youth leader is the whole issue of evangelism. This can often be due to external pressures — church members, your home-group leader, church evangelists, and enthusiastic students all do it all the time, or so it seems. Obviously, they are just good examples of the kinds of people who are strongly into that ministry. We are not all evangelists, but we are all called to be witnesses. So witnessing is needed in our personal lives, and as a youth group. But please be a little cautious in your approach.

Evangelism can be difficult and particularly unrewarding with young people — but it need not be, with gifted and sensitive youth workers and young people alongside. But the crucial question to be asked is: are you running a youth group for young people, or a Christian youth group for followers of Jesus Christ? This seems harsh, so I'll explain what I mean.

Allow me to share a short story with you to illustrate some of the dangers. Imagine the following scenario. You run a small youth group of about eight to ten young people. You feel that the Lord is calling you to evangelise, so you go ahead and find a good venue for a coffee bar. You book every Saturday night for two months, and the church leaders pay the rent. You set things up — a nice kitchen area, with perhaps some biscuits and confectionery; tables and chairs with strategically-placed tracts; a decent sound system playing gentle Christian music. A sign is erected outside inviting young people to come in off the street for a free coffee.

For a while, no one comes in, and the eight young people from your church sit nervously looking at one another, sipping their third cup of coffee and toying with the tracts. Suddenly, a crowd of youngsters arrive. They come in noisily, knocking over tables as they enter the room. You suddenly realise that there are about 30 of them, and that they are looking for fun. They turn up the music, discover it's a Christian tape, and replace with one of their own — heavy metal fills the air. These are seriously non-Christian characters. They light up what you hope are cigarettes and tell dirty stories to one another.

Your attempts to invite them to be quiet while you explain the gospel to them are met with abuse. The members of your youth group understandably cower in the corner of the coffee bar, totally intimidated and afraid to even speak to any of these loud strangers, let alone tell them about the Lord. You decide to press on, and then, during the middle of your second inaudible point, the invaders leave, all at once. The result: you and your youth group have been totally demoralised, and no one has been saved.

When the needs of the unsaved are a higher priority than the needs of the Christians, the resulting imbalance can spell disaster! You will have no idea of who these strangers are; there is no way of contacting them afterwards for future discussion; who knows what they have been smoking, drinking, snorting or injecting? To be perfectly serious, are the members of your church youth group safe? Perhaps the more adventurous girls will be tempted to experiment with these exciting and mysterious young men. Perhaps your young men will be attracted to these brazen, available young girls (there is no perhaps about it).

Allowing the non-Christians to be the majority is, in my opinion, a mistake. Mob rules, no matter what you may say or do. It would be sad if your Christian youth group was broken up by tearaways frightening off Christian youngsters, or if you ended club night with a call to the local police.

It is important that the leaders remain in control of the event, and do not allow things to get out of hand. Any newcomers are given respect as visitors, and in return are expected to behave with politeness, obedience to the rules and to the team members, and to know for sure that they have come into a Christian youth group.

The unbelievers must not be allowed to rule the situation — they must be in the minority, since then they will be overawed by the reality of the faith in their peers. Teach the young people to be themselves even when non-Christians are present. As worship continues, and young people raise their hands, sing heartfelt worship songs to Jesus, pray and share spiritual gifts of words of knowledge, pictures and prophetic insights, the visitors' interest will be aroused. Certainly some will scoff and try to make fun, but they are often unwilling to be the odd man out in this situation.

Given this setting, splitting the group into those who are Christians and those who are visitors can give the person who speaks to the non-Christians the opportunity to draw out discussion and give soul-winning information to them. The Christians are built up in their faith and the youth group grows by salvation, not by invasion.

## Evangelism is the key to growth

Don't hear what I'm not saying. Small may be beautiful, but big is best. Be committed to having a large youth group, and be enthusiastic to ensure that as many people as possible hear the good news and respond to it with faith and repentance. However, I am convinced that the first priority must be the pastoral care of the Christians, who can then be built up in their faith, given a vision and trained to witness to their friends at school.

It was while I was a teenager that I realised that the best person to witness to my schoolmates was me. The Christian that my friends were observing living it out in front of them was me. It was not schools evangelists; not the Christian bands with schools ministries; not Christian sportsmen who visited the town; but me, the person they could observe day in and day out, in all situations. I didn't do a very good job, but I knew it was down to me to be Christ's ambassador in my classroom.

I targeted the ones who seemed most responsive, and eventually one of my friends became a Christian. Others heard the good news, and rejected it. That's not my fault; it's their responsibility before God. Who knows, perhaps they will consider the message of salvation at other times. If I have shared my faith with them, then I have done what Jesus Christ commanded me to do.

*... Go into all the world and preach the good news to all creation* (Mark 16:15).

Fortunately, He never asked me to worry about how others respond to the message, just that I should share it with them.

But I believe that any effectiveness I may have had on my friends was due to the pastoring work of youth leaders in teaching me the truth, and in encouraging me to live it out. To sum up, then, evangelism is best performed the way Jesus did it. With the Samaritan woman, with Nicodemus, and with the rich young ruler, He explained the way of salvation or called them to radical action in a small setting, and He did it personally. His miracles, a lot of His teaching, many healings and deliverances of those possessed by demons happened in public places, with superb didactic effect. And He called many of disciples publicly to follow Him.

But the initial contact was personal. They were attracted to His message by His personality.

Having said all that, I want to underline the value of schools work — after all, I spent six years going into secondary schools in Cardiff and Brighton, teaching classes, taking assemblies and establishing relationships with young people during breaktimes and after school. After a while I realised that the negative atmosphere of assemblies (usually boring, ceremonial, religious and full of notices about detentions and new rules) made them poor places for sharing the good news. I concentrated my time on teaching in the classroom and in befriending young people on the school field.

In my time with the Schools Ministry of Campus Crusade for Christ (now known as the Discovery ministry of Agapé), I learned a great deal about public speaking, putting across the good news to an often hostile audience, and about the value of having a great youth group to which to refer those who expressed an interest.

There are many dangers of which we must beware in schools work. All schools have to hold religious assemblies, and to provide Christian education for every pupil at least once a week. Often headmasters and their heads of department were glad to allow me and my colleagues to take the heat off them by stating an evangelical fundamental view.

Some chose to exercise their right to then 'balance' this by inviting a Buddhist or a Sikh to give their opinion. But in many cases, the teachers involved were delighted to have us in, even if it was just so that they had fewer lessons to prepare!

The lessons were usually integrated into a programme of Social Education, which included such items as sex education, social skills, health education and religious studies. These fit into the structure through talking about sex, pop music, drink and drugs and relating them to the eternal truths of the gospel.

When on school premises, it is important to avoid what is called 'proselytising', which is a general term for promoting your specific beliefs with the intention of converting people and calling for their commitment. We were allowed to share testimony of how we had found Jesus Christ to be the answer and to have dealt effectively with our sin, but we were not allowed to call for a response in the classroom. This would have been ridiculously tacky anyway. The place to call for a response is not while you are all still in the lions' den. We asked them to complete a comment card at the close of our final session, and if students indicated that they were interested to know more, we sent information through the post and followed them up through invitations to a youth meeting or a special evangelistic Bible study.

The bottom line in all this is that the teaching has to be relevant. If the hearers are saved, they only need to hear a good evangelistic talk every so often, while most of the time, they need stronger meat to help them grow in their faith. The unsaved young people will be distractions if we try to ask them to sit through our talk on *Spending time alone with God* or *How to know God's will*. They need to be free to discuss the existence of God, or the reliability of the Bible, or the reason Jesus died.

# Chapter Twelve
# The Psychology of it All

There are several specialist skills needed by the dynamic youth worker, but he or she can be greatly helped to give young people a good time at the club meetings by a programme which takes account of the specific subconscious emotional needs of teenagers. These include: silliness, competition, encouragement, the correct channelling of energy, the building of worthwhile memories, a good relationship with parents and the need for discipline.

School life for teenagers can be pressured, and the difficulties of living at home are on a sliding scale from complicated through downright impossible to disastrous and beyond. A good way to relieve this tension is to provide a great laugh or a really jolly event of some sort. I am a great believer in the silly, the whacky and the enormously daft. That's why I celebrated *Not the Pancake Day* in October (because it wasn't Pancake Day, but wouldn't it be fun to make pancakes, so let's do it anyway!) and why the clocks were turned forward by three and a half hours in order to welcome the New Year at 8.30 p.m.

One Saturday evening the young people were playing football (surprise, surprise) in the church gym, which is small but suitable for teams of three. One team could not find a third player, so I allowed them to play a wastepaper bin as their third player. This was hilarious, since the bin scored a brilliant glancing header, and then disgraced itself by being booked for obstruction. The young people knew this was silly, yet they entered in to the fun and lightness of it all, laying aside their competitiveness for a while as we enjoyed the joke.

Having said that, competitiveness is vital. If your programme does not include opportunities for there to be winners and losers, then change the programme. Far from being a negative experience for the losers, I feel that the reality of competition is a good lesson for the young people to learn. They will win or lose in real life — the bus may be full, or they may get the seat at the front upstairs, so they can put their feet up on the sill; the focus of their affections may agree to going out on a date, or may reject them. These are even more harsh lessons to learn if you've never even been on the losing side in a game of volleyball. Go from the simple, and easy to take, defeats, to the more complicated and important ones.

Championships allow the possibility of giving the winner awards. Look in your Yellow Pages under 'Trophies and Engraving' to find your local trophy shop. Winners can proudly display their medals, cups or plaques on their mantelpieces, and their Grannies will think they are heroes. Kudos and self-esteem go through the roof!

However, competitiveness can be taken too far. When I was at secondary school, I was placed in Mogridge House (all four houses were named after old boys), and house points were awarded for academic excellence, good behaviour (although I only remember them being taken away as a punishment for misbehaviour), and, of course, all forms of sport — football, rugby, tennis, hockey, swimming and cricket. There was even an inter-house tiddlywinks championship once. Privileges were at stake, so the heat was on!

To transfer this sort of team system into a youth group, you could name the houses after patriarchs: *Noah, Abraham, Moses* and *Isaac*; gospel writers: *Matthew, Mark, Luke* and *John*; or your church leaders. Tacky, isn't it? A very poor idea. Too much formalised competition can develop into party spirit. Loosely formed teams for a specific competition, which are rearranged for the next championship, are best; there is enough partisanship within young people for them to cheer on their own side without creating enmity between houses.

Besides that, it would be a shame if *Moses* and *Isaac* had a punch-up, *Mark* lost the final of the quiz because no one knew what 'synoptic' meant, or if *Vicar* had to be disqualified for cheating.

My comments about competition relate mostly to the young men; women sometimes need some encouragement to join in. Enthusiastic female leaders can make a significant difference, as girls will play netball, volleyball or hockey very willingly, given the right jollying along to get things started. I don't need to tell you that once they've got their blood up, they are highly competitive and eager to win at all costs.

# Motivate them into action

Don't let anyone tell you that young people are apathetic; they are not! They are full of energy and drive; it just needs to be channelled properly, or they will pour their efforts into unrighteousness and find the dull routine 'boring'.

The Bible is clear; there is pleasure in sin — if sin were unpleasant, then who would bother? Let's be determined that we are going to give our teenagers no time to fall into sin by providing opportunities for them to give their energies to exciting projects, brilliant games and activities, and quality friendships with each other and their leaders. We have the chance to give them a controlled environment for experiments in life, and for giving them wonderful and extraordinary memories.

I will never forget the day spent running a car-wash, with young people sponsored for the time they spent, and drivers paying a nominal 50p for their car to be hand-washed by a team of damp teenagers. And then there was the day of the Beach Clearance: collecting litter from the seashore, getting our picture in the local paper, and receiving a substantial gift from a local firm for our trouble.

If you have a fashion or a dance workshop, then give the young people a chance to shine a little by having a parade or a demonstration in the meeting before the worship begins. Or have a karaoke, using suitable songs from the charts. You will need to have a video of the song, and a sheet with the words for the teenagers to follow. Provide them with a microphone, and whenever you like, turn off the volume on the TV, and turn up the microphone. Perhaps a panel of judges could give scores, and the winners get a small prize, like a gag.

Alternatively, be aware that plans to provide memories can backfire. I was on a youth holiday a little while ago (some of the pain has faded now), where the leaders wanted everyone to go out for a day's walk on the Quantock Hills in the south-west of England. I was placed with a group, and given the opportunity to get to know some of the young people, to spend time with them and generally to have a nice day. The trouble was that the first thing we had to do, after being dropped 12 miles from the place where we were staying, was to walk up a steep hill. This was the great-grandmother of steep hills, climbing about 4,000ft in about a mile and a half. I could not do it! I had to rest about twice as often as the youngsters, most of whom were fit and healthy. Within ten minutes, I lost sight of them! By the end of the day, I had spent a total of zero minutes with them. My effort had been a complete waste of time!

Special events create special memories. Something as simple as varying the tuck-shop stock can make things seem fresh and new — home-made cakes or even shop-bought lemon-curd doughnuts will sell well and create new interest.

Even taking the radical decision to make the most of the winter weather and go tobogganing — trays can make brilliant makeshift sledges, and bin bags will do — or have a wide game in the dark in the snow, which normally boils down to a jolly game of 'let's all pelt the youth leader at once'. Go on, live a little! Have a warm bath afterwards, though. And perhaps a Lem-Sip. And a week off work. Maybe this isn't such a good idea. It just depends on how committed you are to your youth group ...

# Relating with parents

One of the hardest aspects of being a teenager is finding that your relationship with your parents is changing. Teenagers are no longer children, but they are not yet out of the clutches of their parents.

Equally, things are changing for the hard-pressed parents, as well. I am a youth worker, and not a parent, so I can hardly pontificate about how easy or difficult it is to have teenage offspring! But some do a great job, while others seem to have forgotten about the passing years since they bought roomfuls of Pampers.

We must be full of honour and respect for parents, but realistic about their weaknesses and foibles.

I have found that most parents are grateful for the work I do with their teenagers, although they may have varying degrees of awareness of what goes on at the youth group. They attend the Family Evenings, and take part, on the whole.

But the greatest variation comes in the area of teaching and training. Many parents have, it seems, abandoned the task of teaching their teenagers, and are leaving it to the youth group. I know a few families where prayer times are regular and meaningful, but in the majority of homes such events are rare or memories, if that.

Having moaned a little, I must say that without the support and encouragement we receive from parents, most church youth groups would be unable to continue.

Parents are keen to know that their teenagers are being taught well, and that they enjoy themselves in a safe environment. And they are constantly putting their hands in their pockets when it comes to outings, sleepover events and youth holidays.

I feel that parents' wishes should be obeyed at all times, and that they should be seen to be obeyed. For example, Jon is one of the older members of the youth group, but his parents knew he would not sleep well on the floor of the church gym at one of our sleepover events. So they came to collect him at the end of the evening, and delivered him back again in time for breakfast.

I was concerned that Jon might be given a hard time for this by some of the other lads, but in the end, Jon's enjoyment of the second day vindicated his father's desire that he get a good night's sleep. There were one or two comments made, but they were quickly covered by some joke about being glad to have been spared Jon's snores. Above all, don't dishonour parents, but be careful to be different from them, too.

Youth leaders must be as responsible as parents, but more relaxed; they must be as wise, but prepared to be more silly; they must have authority, but not be heavy-handed; they must be equally interested in every young person, friendly, persuasive, encouraging and prepared to bring discipline as appropriate. Phew!

# And speaking of discipline ...

Most teenagers are prepared to challenge authority, and to push the rules to their limits and beyond. Some young people have never had rules at home, or they have had to cope with inconsistent discipline — some times they are ignored, while at other times they are severely punished for the same offence. Others have never known what the rules are, but have had to discover the boundaries by trial and error. But there are some who think that your youth group would make a good place for a riot, and they are out to make trouble. Dealing with characters like this is a skill acquired through experience. Here are some of the lessons I have learned.

- Have as few rules as possible, but have enough to cover the forms of behaviour you wish to eliminate. Examples: leave light switches alone; don't go outside the building without permission; no loitering in unsupervised areas; treat the building with respect and put litter in the bins provided; obey youth workers; if possible, use the loo before the meeting, and don't consume tuck during the meeting. Display the rules in a prominent place.
- Since these are nearly-adults, use calm reason. Ask them why they are breaking the rules. Take them to where the rules are displayed, and ask them to be reasonable. I have found that it can be helpful to ask the young person if they think I am being fair in asking them to obey the rules. Most agree, albeit reluctantly in some cases.
- Remember to hate the sin, but love the sinner.
- If possible, rebukes should be given in private, away from the gaze of peers. Putting someone down in front of their friends is cruel and unnecessary. However, it can be helpful to name names if they are disrupting the talk.
- Persistent rule-breaking should be punished with a one-week ban, which is backed up by a letter to parents, explaining the offence, and pointing out that the young person is very welcome to return the following week, but is expected to obey the rules. Most parents are supportive, and welcome your help in training their wayward offspring.
- Longer bans may be needed to dissuade troublemakers from continuing. Serious vandalism, e.g. smashing windows, dangerous

activities, e.g. lobbing glass bottles out of an upstairs window at youngsters below, and unsocial behaviour, e.g. stirring up factions, spitting or fighting should all result in robust disciplinary action. Again, a letter to parents explaining the offence(s), the length of the ban and the warm welcome the young person will receive (after the term has elapsed) if they are willing to submit to your authority, is a good idea.

However, please remember that many youngsters swear habitually without even noticing, and that to come down too heavily on this is unfair. Of course, we can ask them to be careful, but give them room to make a few mistakes. Pilfering from the tuck shop can be a problem; again, some have been taught to do this by immoral parents, and a re-training period of grace and mercy may be appropriate. The chances are that my attitude to what is acceptable and what is not is slightly more permissive than many parents; I enjoy a laugh and a caper as much as most young people. This makes me ready and willing to be strong and vigorous when I feel the mark has been overstepped, since my tolerance is generous.

I took a crowd of young people on a Sunday afternoon outing to Gatwick Airport once. They were in high spirits, and since the place was almost deserted, we had a competition to see who could get to the top of the down-escalator first. When members of the public wanted to use the escalator, we let them do so, but there was great fun to be had in being slightly disorderly. We sang *Happy Birthday to You* to one of the young people about six times that afternoon (it wasn't his birthday, but who's counting?) and had a jelly-bean tasting event at the sweet shop. Everyone had fun; even the airport policeman who at first eyed us warily seemed to relax as he saw the spirit of lightness and joy — he knew that we were not about to cause damage or mayhem — and the afternoon was a memorable occasion. I have a sneaky suspicion, however, that one or two parents might have been uncomfortable with the degree of licence I allowed, but the young people knew that I wouldn't let them get away with anything too outrageous. It's a question of mutual trust, setting generous but definite boundaries, and having a good time.

# Chapter Thirteen
# Love 'Em

The subject of love is so important, it deserves to be given specific treatment, and to be the thought with which this book finishes. Here's my advice to those who find themselves disliking youth work, or disliking the young people in their youth group. Forget it. Do something else.

The vital ingredient is love. God never requires something of us without granting to us the ability or power to fulfil His command. He calls us to have love for those in our care; and He gives us the spirit of love with which to love.

> *If I speak in the tongues of men and of angels, but have not love, I am only a resounding gong or a clanging cymbal* (1 Cor. 13:1).
> *For God did not give us a spirit of timidity, but a spirit of power, of love and of self-discipline* (2 Tim. 1:7).

Jesus loves these young people with an everlasting love, and we are His ambassadors, His representatives, and His chosen shepherds of the flock, so let's be certain that we love them with the love of God. Unconditional acceptance of young people is often more than we can manage in the flesh, so let's make sure we are relying on God for help at all times.

One of the most deflating things that happens to me when I'm moving around the building as the activities take place is the attitude of those who have recently joined, or have recently graduated from the younger age group. They have not yet realised that team members are committed to befriending them, so my smile and 'hallo' can often be rebuffed by cursory acknowledgement, or even silence, such as they are used to giving to members of staff at school, where, it seems, the idea is to create as wide an 'us and them' gulf as possible. I recall that, as a teenager, I once said 'hallo' to a new member of staff as he passed me in the corridor. I was called back and so severely rebuked for not saying 'hallo, *sir*', that I never again said anything as I passed members of staff. The insecure new teacher with whom I was genuinely trying to be friendly defended his authority with too much vigour. What a shame!

I want the very opposite, and this is what happens as teenagers stay around at the youth group, and as they grow up in their faith. When I arrive in the middle of a group of youngsters, they at least greet me as if I exist, and those who are particularly friendly are pleased to see me. I have worked hard, and become their friend — a friend they trust and whose company they enjoy, but with the respect due to a youth leader and someone in oversight of them.

It seems beyond belief, but it is possible for tough fourteen-year-old girls to crack their layers of foundation and for their ruby red lips to smile at and greet an adult. It must be the activity of a gracious God in their lives, because I know I am highly honoured that they accept me as just about worthy to tread on the same planet as them.

They say that you're as young as you feel (but that's mostly to disguise the fact that you don't look it). I really enjoy the company of these young people, and while I don't prefer it to the company of people my own age, I would often choose to spend time with teenagers. When Pizza Hut began their amazing offer of 'as much as you can eat for £3', I invited a crowd of youngsters to come with me. We had a great time, eating and laughing, revelling in the carnival atmosphere in the restaurant. The waiters were having a busy but enjoyable time, plying their pizzas to a hungry and receptive crowd of consumers. Everyone had a good deal; by which I mean it was value for money, the waiters didn't have to concentrate on your order, and people stuffed themselves silly. Good conversation and joking helped build relationships as we ate. Three or four lads overdid it a bit (I believe one had to take the next day off school), but they learned their lesson. The whole exercise could have become a homage to gluttony, but it was nevertheless a positive experience.

Another important aspect of being around these teenagers is the whole area of fellowship. It is possible to share truly excellent fellowship with those who are saved. It is often the case that their walk with God is fresh and new, while yours has the benefit of being more mature, but has perhaps become dulled by familiarity. When teenagers pray for me, my spirit is encouraged, I feel strongly loved and I am built up by their conversational style of speaking to God.

Alongside the directly spiritual forms of fellowship, when you are in touch with their tastes and preferences in music, fashion, cosmetics, sport, TV shows or whatever, there are grounds for conversation and for friendly banter. I am thrilled when teenagers ask me what I think of a piece of music — these are my friends, and they value my opinion. I am not perceived to be an outsider, even though I am twice their age. Perhaps all this indicates is that I am immature in my choice of friends, but on the other hand, it might indicate that God has blessed me abundantly with the ability to befriend teenagers, who, as we have already discussed, need friends. They need acceptance and love from adults, since some adults fear them, some belittle them, and the rest  give them a wide berth.

## Conclusion

Sometimes the love has to stretch a long way, like the day I saw eighteen-year-old Steve (not his real name) in possession of joints. After praying and taking advice, I told his father, a prominent member of the church, who then confronted Steve. I later heard that he had denied it, and his father told me I must have been mistaken. But I knew what I had seen. Time passed, and Steve was offered the chance to live away from home with some other Christians for a few weeks. Steve's father felt this would be good, since it would give Steve time away from the pressures of family life, and bring him under the influence of strong Christians.

Just before Steve left, he lashed out at me. 'You're the one who has caused this. I'm being thrown out my family, thanks to you.' I knew this was unfair, but what could I do? It was out of my hands.

Several weeks went by, while Steve discovered exciting new horizons. I was slightly fearful of his return, in case he was still angry with me, but the reverse was the case. We met, and he graciously apologised to me. 'Yes, they were spliffs you saw. I had to lie to avoid upsetting my father any more. But while I was away, I suddenly realised how much Jesus loves me. I understood for the first time that He had given everything for my sake.' Going away had given Steve the chance to understand the good news without the pressures of family or youth leaders. The salvation which came to Steve while he was away has remained as strong as ever, and he has completely given up his involvement with drugs.

It cost me something to have to accuse Steve before his father; there was a cost when his father told me that he believed Steve's denial, and that I must have been mistaken; Steve's angry comment was painful. But it was worth it when Steve came up to me and thanked me for my part in the process God used to give him salvation. I may not have handled the situation as well as possible, but God knew that my heart attitude was one of love and willingness to stand up for what I knew to be the truth.

Let's commit ourselves before the Lord to do our best to love young people with a pure and Godly love, which builds them up and brings them towards salvation, and maturity in their walk with Jesus Christ.

Perhaps you have been in youth work for some time, and are running out of energy or ideas. I would encourage you to take a short break from youth work (perhaps two or three months) and then to come back with renewed vigour and enthusiasm. Sometimes I have seen youth workers communicate more by their tiredness than by their words, and this is self-defeating, since the young people are very sensitive to moods and attitudes. But when youth workers return to the work refreshed, they are once again effective for the Lord. Even if taking a break means that the young people will be less than adequately served for a while, I believe that the long-term implications of running yourself into the ground or continuing to work hard with no desire to do so will have a negative effect on the teenagers.

As called and anointed youth workers, let's determine that we will draw on spiritual resources to remain fresh and joyful in our work. Let's devote ourselves to encourage one another constantly. If you work alone, or with a very small team, take the trouble have fellowship with other youth workers at conferences or at inter-church gatherings. It is good to discuss different ways of doing things, but please be careful to build one another up in the work, rather than just pointing out errors or failings. We all have weaknesses; it's easier to work on them when we know our strengths are acknowledged and appreciated.

And let's be whole-heartedly dedicated to sharing our lives in fun and fellowship with lively, excitable and dynamic young people. They are part of the church of today, but the church of tomorrow will be shaped by the input you give to their lives. Show them love and acceptance, teach them to be disciplined and to have spiritual expectancy, and lead them into biblical truth and worship. Be a good and faithful servant of God; be filled with the Spirit; be a positive role-model. Let them see Jesus in you.